LIGHTS OF PROPHECY
אורות הנבואה

Bezalel Naor

Published by the Union of Orthodox Jewish Congregations of America, 45 West 36th Street, New York, NY 10018.

Library of Congress Catalog Card Number:
90-070976

ISBN 1-879016-00-1

Produced by Olivestone Print Communications, Inc.

PRINTED IN THE UNITED STATES OF AMERICA

Contents

Hebrew Section follows page 56

אם לא תדעי לך היפה בנשים, צאי־לך בעקבי הצאן ורעי את גדיותיך על משכנות הרעים.

שיר השירים א,ח

כנסייתי ועדתי היפה בנשים, בשאר אומות, איכה תרעי ותנצלי מיד המציקים לך, להיות ביניהם ולא יאבדו בניך, התבונני בדרכי אבותיך הראשונים שקבלו תורתי ושמרו משמרתי ומצותי, ולכו בדרכיהם, ואף בשכר זאת תרעי גדיותיך אצל שרי האומות וכן אמר ירמיה [ירמיה לא,כ] הציבי לך ציונים [שמי לך תמרורים] שתי לבך למסלה [דרך הלכת, שובי בתולת ישראל, שבי אל עריך אלה].

רש"י שם

Publication of this book was made possible by the munificence of Mr. and Mrs. Robert M. Schottenstein of Cleveland, Ohio, in the fervent hope that it open the eyes of our people to the beauty and depth which lie within our sacred tradition. Mr. Schottenstein has committed himself and his family to living up to the noble example of his forebears, whose piety, generosity and humanity have become legend. May Hashem yitbarach grant Reb Yehoshua, she-yihye, his dear wife, Chaya, she-tihye and their wonderful sons, Yitshak Eizik, Efraim Eliezer and Avraham Yonah, she-yihyu, the blessing reserved for those who, out of a sense of love and devotion to their people, strengthen Torah learning and observance:

ברוך אשר יקים את דברי התורה הזאת לעשות אותם!

Preface

Some of us cannot believe how far we American Orthodox Jews have come—yet, when we compare ourselves to our forebears, it is difficult to appreciate how far we have fallen. Essentially, the Jewish People is a people of the spirit—the foundation of our people is Torah, the quest for truth and a life of spirituality. Yet, if the fact be known, despite contemporary Jews' fierce loyalty to Torah and the commandments, despite our exciting progress in reestablishing the basic institutions of the Torah community, our head and our mind are still elsewhere.

The founder of Hasidism, R. Yisrael Ba'al Shem Tov, once said that a human being is to be found not where his feet are standing, but where his thoughts are. Most American Orthodox Jews, even when we are standing in the synagogue or the Beth Medrash, are thinking about something else: business, family, the stock market. Basically we attempt to master the world, not to master ourselves—to link our hearts and minds to God and the world of eternity and spirit, where we must concentrate on developing and refining ourselves, our personalities and our sensitivities.

This small book is an attempt to recreate an awareness of where our minds and thoughts should be. It is an introduction to the world of Jewish prophecy, a world which speaks to us today much as it spoke to our fathers and mothers in the past.

Rabbi Pinchas Stolper

Foreword

Is it possible that our hedonistic era may witness a revival of the spiritual and even the prophetic aspect of Judaism?

Was the loss of prophecy at the beginning of the Second Commonwealth total, or did lesser levels of divine inspiration and experience continue to thrive after full-blown prophecy had ceased?

Does the emphasis, or perhaps over-emphasis, on the intellectual side of Judaism in some circles, convey a one-sided and incomplete picture of the full dimensions of post-prophetic Jewish History?

These are some of the themes that concerned Rabbi Bezalel Naor when he compiled this provocative collection of short pieces from a wide range of traditional sources.

Recent years have seen a greater focus on externals. This represents, at least in part, a defense reaction to the inroads of the dominant culture. However, it may also mask or compensate for a lack of inner depth and spirituality. One of the effects of this situation is the existence of a disturbingly large number of young people from religious homes who are not 'turned on' to Yiddishkeit.

Simultaneous with the above-mentioned hedonism and superficiality one detects a contemporary yearning for greater spirituality. Rabbi Naor's intriguing and inspiring collection is a symptom of that yearning.

May it also serve as a catalyst for a reawakening and a renewal of the Jewish spirit.

Matis Greenblatt
Literary Editor, *Jewish Action*

INTRODUCTION

Introduction

The work before us is a selection of sources pertaining to the topic of Prophecy. Some, such as *Guide of the Perplexed,* by Maimonides, are classics of Jewish Philosophy. Others, such as *Interpretation of Dreams,* by R. Shelomo Almoli and *Conditions of the Soul for Attainment of Hasidut,* by R. Menahem Eckstein, are little-known works by obscure authors. All are situated within the mainstream of Orthodox tradition. As in any meaningful compilation, the editor brings to bear his own interpretation of events. The message is conveyed by juxtaposing passages. Translation of all material quoted is the editor's own; it may be that it too reflects certain foci which are peculiar to the editor's perspective. For the sake of objectivity, the Hebrew original of all texts has been provided, so that the reader need not rely on the editor's judgement in such matters.

I

The first section, "Prophecy/Past" speculates as to the reason for prophecy's disappearance. According to the oldest source cited, the medieval German *Sefer Hasidim,* prophecy was provided by God to counterbalance the attraction of paganism; with the eradication of

1

idolatry, it became superfluous! At first glance, one is astounded by what would seem unabashed reductionism. However, one must recall that the institution of prophecy as originally chartered in Deuteronomy 18:9-22 may be read as just such a displacement of indigenous Canaanite necromancy. [See especially verse 14 and *Sifré ad locum*, cited in Nahmanides' commentary verse 9. Cf. Nahmanides, *Derashat Torat Ha-Shem Temimah,* in C.B. Chavel's *Kitvey R. Moshe ben Nahman* (Jerusalem, 5723) I, 149-150; R. Nissim b. Reuben Gerondi, *Derashot Ha-Ran* (Feldman ed., Jerusalem, 5737) XI, 204-205; Maimonides, Introduction to *Commentary on Mishnah* and R. Shneur Zalman of Liady, *Tanya* IV, 22. However, see the objection of R. Yosef Albo, *'Iqqarim* III, 8.] We might just mention *en passant* the controversy Maimonides triggered when he subjected the sacrificial cult to this form of reductionism. [See Maimonides, *Guide* III, 32; Nahmanides, Leviticus 1:9; R. Yom Tov b. Abraham of Seville (Ritba), *Sefer ha-Zikaron* (Kahana ed., Jerusalem, 5743) 73-78; Abrabanel, introduction to Leviticus.] At stake here is whether reinstitution of prophecy (or the sacrificial cult) in a more advanced civilization would be "anachronistic".

The Vilna Gaon (1720-1797) too, in his laconic style, connects the cessation of prophecy to the eradication of idolatry—without providing us the key to understand this interdependence.

The Gaon's rival, R. Shneur Zalman of Liady (1745-1813), explains the phenomenon by saying that the Divine Presence and the proliferation of idolatrous cults are two sides of the same coin: belief in the supernatural. The transition from First to Second Temples meant the shifting of view from God to Man, from deicentric to anthropocentric.

R. Zadok ha-Kohen of Lublin (1823-1900) outlines the

history of the First and Second Temples in quite similar fashion. The major difference between R. Shneur Zalman and R. Zadok's descriptions lies in their portrayals of the Second Commonwealth. Whereas for R. Shneur Zalman, the passage which most accurately characterizes the period is that in the Tractate *Yoma* (21b), which treats of the five symbols of divine intervention lacking in the Second Temple ("ark, fire, divine presence *(shekhinah)*, divine inspiration *(ruah ha-qodesh)*, and Urim and Thummim")—for R. Zadok, the era is epitomized by the words of the *Pirqey Hekhalot*: "Said Rabbi Ishmael, so said Rabbi Aqiva in the name of Rabbi Eliezer the Great: 'From the time Torah was given to Israel, its splendor and glory, etc. were not revealed until the last (Second) Temple [even though] the divine presence was not manifest therein'" [*Pirqey Hekhalot Rabbati,* end chapter 28, published in Wertheimer's *Batei Midrashot* (Jerusalem, 5728) Volume One; see R. Zadok ha-Kohen, *Taqqanat ha-Shavin* 6:24 and *Mahshevot Haruz* 71d].

In this writer's opinion, one of the most fascinating points of R. Zadok's historiography is his isolation of the encounter of Alexander the Great and Simon the Just (recorded in *Talmud Bavli, Yoma* 69a) as being the symbolic passage from the Old Age of Prophecy to the New Age of Reason. On one side, we have Simon the Just, last of the Men of the Great Assembly (*Mishnah, Avot* 1:2) whom R. Zadok (based on *Pirqey Hekhalot*) credits with the elevation of the Oral Law to a position of supremacy in Jewish life. From the opposite side, approaches Alexander of Macedonia, student of the preeminent rationalist Aristotle. The dating is breathtakingly precise. A generation earlier in Greece, taught Plato, whose philosophy is yet interspersed with elements of mysticism and mythology. In Israel, that very legislative body known as the Men of the Great Assembly, had been graced by the membership of the last prophets. Truly the generation of Simon and Alexander was the great watershed. The essential difference between the philosophies of Plato and his disciple Aristotle is made most explicit in the quote from *Orot ha-Emunah* of Rav Kook.

[Parenthetically, both R. Zadok and Rav Kook regard Maimonides as the *tiqqun* or correction of Aristotelian rationalism. This is but one of many instances where the positions of R. Zadok and Rav Kook coincide, as scholars have already noted.

One also observes the overall fairhandedness of the presentation. Jerusalem and Athens are viewed as parallel civilizations which developed independently. Refreshingly, we have here none of the ethnocentrism which supposes an Israelite source for Greek philosophy. (See Josephus Flavius, *Contra Apion*; R. Yehuda ha-Levi, *Kuzari* I, 63 and II, 66; et al.) It is a tribute to Maimonides that he (despite what some try to read into the *Guide* I, 71—see e.g. R. Pinhas Elijah b. Meir (Hurwitz) of Vilna, *Sefer ha-Berit ha-Shalem* I, 20:32) never entertained such a thought. On the contrary, in his introduction to the *Commentary on Mishnah*, he maintained that "the sages of the early peoples neither saw the prophets nor heard their words." There follows immediately a reference to Aristotle. (See *Mishnah 'im Perush ha-Rambam*, Kapah ed. (Jerusalem, 5723) *Seder Zera'im, Haqdamah*, 23a.)

A final aside: R. Zadok employs the term *hokhmat yewanit* in the sense of Greek Philosophy. However, from a critical stance, it is highly unlikely the Rabbis of the Talmud ever intended that meaning. See Rashi, *Menahot* 64b and R. Isaac b. Sheshet, *She'elot u-Teshuvot Ribash*, no. 45; also Maimonides' commentary to *Mishnah*, end *Sotah*; and most recently, Dov Schwartz's article, *"Hokhmat Yewanit"*, Sinai, Sivan-Tammuz, 5749.]

But all this is more descriptive phenomenology than

analytic etiology. In the two pieces quoted subsequently (*Divrei Soferim* 21b and *Resisay Layla* 7b-c), R. Zadok likens idolatry to a filter which shields the blinding rays of prophecy. Prophecy was possible only because there was idolatry to impugn it. The removal of idolatry by the Men of the Great Assembly threatened to destroy human free will, which would now be exposed to the full impact of prophetic revelation. At that point, the Lord extinguished the overwhelming light of prophecy, in order to safeguard man's free will. [So Rav Dessler (1891-1954) explains the meaning of R. Zadok's rather cryptic words.] In every generation, the Master of the Universe insures the preservation of free will, by maintaining a perfect balance of power between Good and Evil.

Rav Kook (1865-1935), titan of Jewish thought, combines the theory of Maimonides (*Guide* II, 36-37; cf. *Tiqquney Zohar*, beg. *Tiqqun* 18 and *Tiqqun* 30), which views prophecy as a function of the imaginative faculty, with the finding of the *Sefer Hasidim* (and the Vilna Gaon) that the disappearance of prophecy is linked to the eradication of idolatry. Rav Kook observes that both these phenomena, i.e. prophecy and idolatry, are dependent on an active imagination. Judaism sans prophecy, tends to be a religion of reason rather than of imagination. At the root of both prophecy and idolatry, lie vision and the desire for some substantive contact with the divine. In the case of prophecy, the vision is restricted to the mind's eye, whereas in idolatry it finds expression in the plastic arts. As for substantive contact, Rav Kook's *mot-cle* is instructive: *tokhen* or "content". Only prophetic religion can supply this type of "content". The religion of pure reason is too abstract to accommodate all dimensions of a human being. [Cf. *'Arpiley Tohar* (Jerusalem, 5743) 10.] Finally, Rav Kook intimates that in our own time there are indications that the long-dormant imagination is being reawakened, which augurs well for the future restoration of prophecy. (More in this regard in Section Three: "Prophecy/Future".)

II

Section Two, entitled "Prophecy/Present", discusses what form divine inspiration has taken since the disappearance of classical prophecy, which was distinguished by outright visions. In this connection, two sayings of the Rabbis are most significant: "Since the day the Temple was destroyed, prophecy was taken from the prophets and given to the sages" (*Bava Batra* 12a); and "With the demise of the last prophets, Haggai, Zechariah and Malachi, the Holy Spirit departed from Israel; nevertheless, they would employ the *bat qol* (divine voice)" (*Sanhedrin* 11a). In order to be receptive to these indirect modes of divine communication, one may have to alter certain ground-assumptions of one's theory of knowledge, or epistemology.

The first mode left to us, is the so-called "prophecy of sages." [In subsequent literature this would no longer be referred to as *nevuah* or prophecy (reserved for an external stimulus), but rather as an internal *ruah ha-qodesh* (divine inspiration). See Nahmanides, *Hiddushei Ramban, Bava Batra* 12a; R. Elijah Gaon of Vilna, *Be'ur ha-Gra,* Isaiah 5:7; R. Hayyim Vital, *Sha'arei Qedusha* III, 6-7; and R. Pinhas Elijah b. Meir (Hurwitz) of Vilna, *Sefer ha-Berit ha-Shalem,* First Introduction, Preface, I, 1:1, II, 9:3 and 11:1,3.] Though God does not speak to us directly any more, the Sages of Israel, who immerse themselves in Torah learning, are able to reach mystical or quasi-mystical states of rapture, whereby they perceive prophetic meaning in the Torah itself. A most pronounced form of such inspiration, would be the case of Rabbi Yosef Caro (1488-1575), who, while studying Mishnah, would be seized with automatic speech gushing from his vocal chords, addressing him with the words, "I am the Mishnah speaking through your mouth." The genius of the *Mishnah,* or *Maggid,* would then launch into lengthy soliloquy. [See the extensive literature on *Maggidism,* especially R. Hayyim of Volozhin's introduction to his master, the Gaon of Vilna's commentary on *Sifra di-Zeni'uta* and R. Zadok ha-Kohen, *Dover Zedeq,* 81b.] This is a very extreme example. We may rest assured that subtler, less shocking types of Torah inspiration exist. The example of the Talmud (Bava Batra 12b) is that of a sage who independently arrives at a law which had already been revealed to Moses on Sinai. The Rebbe of Piaseczno (*Mevo ha-She'arim,* Chapter Two) cites as an example of this type of divine inspiration, the fact that sometimes one intuits that one can contribute some original insight in a certain area of Torah scholarship— which afterwards proves true—though rationally there was no reason to have assumed such.

We should also mention the concept of "taking counsel from the Torah". "Our master (the Gaon of Vilna) revealed the secret how to take counsel from the Torah. One should learn with great enthusiasm until one seems to be learning *lishmah* (for Torah's sake) and then one should consider the project, whether to go ahead with it or not. That which comes to mind at that moment, one should follow—that is the counsel of the Torah" [*Orhot Hayyim—Keter Rosh,* by R. Asher ha-Kohen of Tiktin, par. 6 and commentary *Oholei Hayyim* there]. Besides this more abstract form of "counseling", the text of the Torah serves in a mantic capacity: one opens at random to a page, which contains the "message". Known popularly today as the "*Goral ha-Gera*" ("the Gaon of Vilna's Lottery"), R. Hayyim Yosef David Azulai mentions earlier Sefardic luminaries who were wont to consult the Torah in this manner (see *Birkhey Yosef, Yoreh De'ah* 179:8). [See further *'Emeq ha-Neziv, Sifré, Shoftim* 31 (Deut. 18:14) s.v. *lekha nitnah;* Rabbi Joseph D. Epstein *shlita, Mizvat ha-'Ezah* (New York, 1983) p.28, n.39; and R. Elhanan Adler, "Impermissible Superstitious Practices", *Beit Yosef Shaul* (New York, 5749) p. 183, n.20.] Rav Kook contemplated composing a work ("for which one volume and one generation might prove insufficient"!) to demonstrate how the sundry systems of thought from time immemorial, may be unified by a single linchpin. To a degree, this wish was fulfilled in the *Qol ha-Nevuah* ("Voice of Prophecy") of his close disciple, R. David Cohen, the "Nazir" (?-1972). As R. Aharon Lichtenstein (1933–   ) has pointed out, the latter stretches the concept of prophecy so that, in a sense, it enfolds all Jewish learning. But in the selections, I have shown that just such a position was adopted by Nahmanides (1194-1270), R. Shelomo Almoli (before 1485—after 1542) and R. Menahem Mendel of Lubavitch ("Zemah Zedeq") (1789-1866), all of whom cited the Gemara *Bava Batra* (12a) as their prooftext. [A relatively recent statement of this position is to be found in R. Kalonymos Kalman Shapiro's *Mevo ha-She'arim,* pp. 6b-7a. See especially the footnote there.]

Indeed, the issue raised by Rav Lichtenstein is a most sensitive one and not to be treated lightly. Once one opens the definition of prophecy to embrace more than the classic prophets of yore, where does it end? Does one draw the line with Torah and Torah sages (the position adopted by Nahmanides and Zemah Zedeq)? [R. Nahman's "Zaddiq" is a variation on the theme. In another passage in *Liqqutey Moharan* (II, 8:8) he attributes semi-prophetic ability to the *Manhig* or Leader. It is not my intention at this time to probe the phenomenon known as *Zaddiqism,* and to determine to what degree the concept of the *Zaddiq* is merely an extension of the older Talmudic concept of the "Hakham", beyond which *Zaddiqism* is a radical innovation of the Hasidic movement. Historically, *Zaddiqism* is usually thought to be the creation of R. Elimelekh of Lyzhansk, Galicia (1717-1787). Interestingly enough, R. Nahman, inhabitant of the Ukraine, lauds this distinctly *Galician* phenomenon. Did he have the teachings of Rebbe Elimelekh in mind? This should be the subject of historical investigation.] Could the term *prophecy* used in this very loose sense extend to wisdom per se (not necessarily Torah wisdom) as R. Shelomo Almoli would seem to suggest? Seen from this perspective, the Divine Flow ripples through all human intellect. Certainly R. Shelomo Almoli's radical view is a minority opinion. [However, see *Seder Eliyahu Rabbah,* IX; R. Hayyim Vital, *Sha'arei Qedusha* 3:7; and R. Pinhas Elijah of Vilna, *Sefer ha-Berit ha-Shalem,* II, 10:1.]

The second mode of post-prophetic divine communication is the *"bat qol"*. While we tend to think of *bat qol* as some sort of supernatural voice ringing out from heaven, upon closer examination of the Talmudic sources (particularly the Jerusalem Talmud) we find that divination based on common everyday conversation, in the right circumstances was considered "following the *bat qol"*. Thus R. Zadok ha-Kohen develops the theory of the *"qala de-hadra"* or divine echo which reverberates throughout existence. As he expresses the thought so boldly: "All human speech is but the echo of God!" At the end of R. Zadok's rather lengthy essay, the two types of inspiration—scriptural and aural—dovetail in the "Echo of (successive generations of) Torah (architects)".

[Here it must be stated that after great lengths to link

the two phenomena of *bat qol* and the Oral Law (see *Dover Zedeq* 72d), a few pages later the dynamic R. Zadok reverses himself and declares: "Truthfully, the wisdom of the Oral Law is not called *bat qol* (divine voice), but rather *ruah ha-qodesh* (divine inspiration)" [ibid, 74b]. In the final analysis, only *ruah ha-qodesh* has survived to the present, not *bat qol* proper, which was restricted to the period of the Second Temple. See Nahmanides, *Derashat Torat Ha-Shem Temimah*, in Chavel's *Kitvey Ramban* I, 148-149; *Zohar* I, 238a; and my essay "*Shalosh Mishmarot Havé Ha-Layla*", in *Eshel Avraham*, pp. 11-12, appended to B. Naor, *Hassagot ha-Rabad le-Mishneh Torah* (second edition, Jerusalem, 5745). We must differentiate between the classic phenomenon of *bat qol* which was a more direct, distinct form of divine communication, and the divination which was a more colloquial form of *bat qol*, properly referred to as *simanim* or signs. The latter phenomenon does persist to the present.

Regarding R. Zadok's theory of the subjective *bat qol* perceived by individuals in their hearts, see also *Peri Zaddiq* (Lublin, 5694) V, 111d-112c. For a brief summary of the classic opinions concerning the nature of the *bat qol*, see R. Yizhaq Arieli's *Einayim le-Mishpat, Berakhot* 3a and *Makkot* 23b. R. Reuven Margaliot, whose breadth of scholarship is unsurpassed, included a section on "Bat Qol" in his edition of *She'elot u-Teshuvot min ha-Shamayim* (Jerusalem, 5717).]

Though R. Nahman of Bratslav (1772-1811) does not specify the medium of sound, his perception of a world laden with hints *(remazim)*, certainly bears remarkable similarity to R. Zadok's teaching. [Chronologically, R. Nahman preceded R. Zadok. To what degree R. Zadok's work is influenced by R. Nahman, is as yet unresolved. The fact that R. Zadok penned notes to R. Nahman's

Sefer ha-Middot, means only that he held the work and (one must assume) its author in esteem, not that he was a Bratslaver *hasid,* as some of R. Nahman's present-day followers would contend.] According to R. Nahman, God is constantly sending Man cues.

III

The third section, "Prophecy/Future", attempts to penetrate the essence of prophetic consciousness, in order to understand from the human end (not omitting the other, divine side of the equation) what conditions must be met in order to precipitate prophecy. Maimonides' *Guide* serves as the basis for discussion. Maimonides (1135-1204) attempted to relate the phenomenon of prophecy to a physical propensity, the imaginative faculty. He was attacked on this score by Don Isaac Abrabanel (1437-1508) who in his lengthy commentary to the *Guide* (II, 36), rejected this supposed physiological basis for prophecy and militated for its purely metaphysical, God-given nature. This controversy recalls the entire Mind-Body problem which continues in full force in intellectual circles to the present day.

Maimonides goes on to say that the prophet represents the perfection of reason and imagination. If either of these ingredients is missing, the result is a personality other than the prophetic. Reason, without the buoyancy of imagination, produces the prosaic scholar. Fancy, deprived of the grounding influence of reason, gives rise to charlatans of every possible description. The prophetic mentality is the happy marriage of Reason and Imagination.

Finally, Maimonides traces throughout the annals

of Jewish history the dependence of prophetic ability on healthy, functioning imagination. Maimonides does not attribute the disappearance of prophecy to the legendary action of the Men of the Great Assembly, but rather to the deleterious effects of exile. He concludes his analysis on a hopeful note: Just as Exile enervated imagination and thus brought about the cessation of prophecy, Redemption will reactivate imagination and predispose the restoration of prophecy.

R. Nahman of Bratslav (1772-1811) in kabbalistic rather than philosophical jargon, gives us an experiential taste of the dialectic of the Infinite and the Finite. [To transfer for a moment to yet a third tradition within Judaism, never was the thought expressed more succinctly than by the founder of the Mussar movement, Rabbi Israel Salanter (1810-1883): "Man is free in his imagination and a prisoner of his intellect". (Cf. *Tiqquney Zohar* (*Tiqqun* 6), "*a King imprisoned in chambers* (Song of Songs 7:6)—in the chambers of the mind".)] To reason has fallen the task of reining in the mind, even as it attempts to storm the heavens. There is within the mind an organizing principle (termed by R. Nahman, *Keter* or "Crown") which is able to order and make sense of the chaotic. Out of this dynamic tension arise "Palaces of Infinite Light", a seeming contradiction in terms, forged of the contradiction which is Man, "body from below and soul from above" (Rashi, Gen. 2:7, s.v. *vayyipah be-apav*).

R. Nahman's student, R. Nathan of Nemirov (1780-1845), in a truly seminal piece in *Liqqutey Halakhot,* assigns imagination to the pagan world and reason to Israel. Of course, Jews too possess imagination, but they strive to conquer it with reason. Left on its own, the imaginative faculty fosters idolatrous leanings. Viewed psychologically, Judaism's anathema on graven images,

is an outcry against unredeemed imagination. R. Nathan
does not mention prophecy, but it would seem fair to assume he would view prophecy as a successful dialectic
of imagination and reason. [Cf. *Liqqutey Moharan* II,
8:7, where R. Nahman declares prophecy to be the
clarification and rectification of the imaginative faculty.]
The prophets of Israel, rather than being swept away
by the momentum of their visions, were able to uplift
them by virtue of their prodigious intellectual gifts, thus
stripping the images of their gross corporeality and
returning them to the Invisible One.

If we were to probe even deeper the underpinnings
of prophetic ability, we might find the "imaginative
faculty" to be the cascade of a reservoir of creative sexual
energy. The Kabbalists spoke of the two *sefirot "Nezah"*
and *"Hod"* as being the supernal source of prophecy [see
Zohar, I, 21b; II, 140b, 257b; III, *Raya Mehemna* 68b,
236b, 307a; *Tiqquney Zohar,* 2a; *Tiqquney Zohar Hadash*
(Vilna, 1867) 7b]. R. Zadok astutely observes that
inasmuch as *"Nezah"* and *"Hod"* refer to the two thighs,
what in fact is being said, is that there is a sexual
component to prophecy. Thus, only those who are ex-
tremely moral in their sexual comportment, channeling
their creative energy through conduits of *qedusha* (holiness), merit authentic prophecy. [In the remainder of that
passage in the text, R. Zadok holds up Samuel, "Master
of the Prophets", as a shining example of sexual purity.
See *Zohar* I, 216.]

Rav Kook makes the equally astute observation that
it can hardly be coincidental that the same movement—
Hasidism—which championed emotionality and imaginative service of the Lord through song and dance, etc.,
demanded of its adherents ritual ablutions far in excess
of the strict letter of the law. Reintroduction in Judaism
of the ancient imaginative element, presents problems.

Once the great reservoir of sexual energy is undammed, extreme caution must be exercised to insure that it flow evenly in the direction of the divine. Sensitive to this problem, Hasidism, along with renewed emphasis on enthusiastic worship (conducive to divine inspiration), revived the practice of daily immersion in the *miqveh* (ritual bath). Shifting the emphasis from the rational to the imaginative and emotional, from mind to body, requires commensurate attention to the physical state of purity. As a postscript one might add, there is no branch of Hasidism more imaginative than that of Bratslav (where storytelling was promoted to supreme significance), and none more emphatic in its insistence on sexual purity.

In yet another piece in *Orot,* Rav Kook comments on the direction modern society has taken, with its stimulation of the imagination to the detriment of philosophical speculation. To borrow Maimonidean terminology, while "the class of men of science engaged in speculation" has receded to the periphery of the contemporary scene, those who make their livelihood by dispensing the products of imagination are in the forefront of the arena. By a paradoxical twist which is so typically Rav Kook, we are assured that this is the divine plan at work, scheming to reconstruct the impaired imaginative faculty in preparation for the Messiah's advent. Inasmuch as the return of prophecy is part of the Messianic agenda, reactivation of imagination must also be included therein.

The stimulation (or overstimulation) of the artistic media affects society en masse. There is however, a subtler, but no less significant, development within the ivory towers of Academia. Previously theology was considered one of the sciences, such as mathematics or physics. Many would boast that the crowning achievement of the Kantian revolution was the freeing of science from the yoke of metaphysics. Rav Kook, again with that touch of irony for which he is famous, throws out a challenge to those who would gloat at Theology's defeat. When Theology was banished from the mainstream of academic life, it was far from defeated. On the contrary, Theology merely went underground, to resurface at a future date as full-fledged Prophecy. Science may have thrown off the yoke of Theology, but thereby Theology too broke the shackles of rationalism which fettered its free spirit and imagination.

While Rav Kook was content with sociological commentary, an obscure contemporary, R. Menahem Eckstein of Vienna, actually published a manual of practical exercises designed to stretch the imagination beyond our tragically circumscribed picture of existence. His *Conditions of the Soul for Attainment of Hasidut* is in many ways the forerunner of the well-known film, *Cosmic Zoom*. [Certainly noteworthy in this regard, are the printed works of the martyred Rebbe of Piaseczno, R. Kalonymos Kalmish Shapiro (1889-1943): *Hovat ha-Talmidim, Hakhsharat ha-Avrekhim* and *Mevo ha-She'arim*. Both Rabbis Eckstein and Shapiro provide exercises for the stimulation of the *koah ha-medameh* (imaginative faculty) to the end of Hasidic devotion; however, the Piaseczner's tracts are full of references to prophetic theory per se (beyond the framework of Hasidism). At one point, he says in a most frank manner: "We desire to unleash a spark of the vision of the *sons of prophets* which is within us" [*Hakhsharat ha-Avrekhim* (Jerusalem, 5726) 30a; see too the lengthy note on pages 10a-b]. I am confident that future writers will find a fitting memorial for this truly great master.]

IV

The final section of our work deals with "visionary cosmologies". Prophecy concerns not only prediction of the future, but also formulation of a comprehensive vision of reality. Such a vision was that of Ezekiel, referred to in rabbinic literature as *Ma'aseh Merkavah*, the Work of the Chariot.

What is less known, but equally important, is that the great sixteenth century Safed mystic, Rabbi Isaac Luria [referred to as "Ari"] (1534-1572), who revolutionized Kabbalah (and indirectly, all Jewish thought and living) to this day, was also privy to such an ecstatic vision. We have this on the authority of none other than Rabbi Moshe Hayyim Luzzato (1707-1746) and R. Zadok ha-Kohen.

[For the sake of intellectual honesty, it must be stated that in other passages of his voluminous work, R. Zadok seems to say the exact opposite, namely that the Ari, in contradistinction to the prophets, reached his breakthroughs rationally, not by ecstatic visions. "It is known in the writings of the Ari that he revealed many things which are beyond the ken of the prophets, as he wrote himself in *Sha'ar ha-Nevuah*. Not that the prophets were incapable of such attainment. They could reach those levels, but only intellectually and not by prophetic inspiration (which in their day was esteemed more highly than intellectual achievement)" [*Mahshevot Harutz*, 71c-d]. "It is known that the Ari related things concerning the higher worlds which, in his own judgement transcended the reach of the prophets ... But they apprehended through vision . . . while he apprehended through intellect" [*Resisay Layla*, 79d]. This requires further investigation. Cf. R. Kalonymos Kalman Shapiro of

Piaseczno, *Mevo ha-She'arim* (Jerusalem, 5726) 13a-15a, and Maharal of Prague, *Gevurot Ha-Shem*, First Introduction.]

Closer to our own day, Shem Tov Geffen (1857-1927), mathematical theoretician *par excellence*, in a most revealing entry in his memoirs, shares with us something of his own cosmic experience.

Summary

What was the essence of prophecy which was lost and has not been recovered to this day? It was the Voice, the *Qol*. That awesome sound which reverberated throughout the four hundred parasangs of the Holy Land, was stopped up in a "lead container" and has never been heard again with that same force and intensity.

What sort of voice was it? The philosophers contend it was an internal voice heard within the mind and thus inaudible to others (see R. Pinhas Elijah of Vilna, *Sefer ha-Berit ha-Shalem* I, 17:13-14; II, 10:1). The kabbalists on the other hand, assign such internal voices to a lower level of prophecy; in the higher form of prophecy, the voice is an external manifestation which addresses the prophet (ibid). [See the earlier discussion in Maimonides' *Guide* II, end chapter 45. According to Maimonides, the voice of lesser prophets was the product of the imaginative faculty, whereas the voice Moses heard was emitted from between the two cherubs above the Ark. Some commentators claim Maimonides used the term "two cherubs above the Ark" as a figure for the intellect (see Efodi and Shem Tov). Abrabanel rejects this figurative reading. Crescas is undecided.] R. Zadok ha-Kohen of Lublin adopts an intermediate position: the voice may be heard objectively, but it is the prophet's own voice resounding from his vocal chords! (*Dover Zedeq*, 81b, based on R. Hayyim Vital, beg. *Sha'ar Ruah ha-Qodesh*).

[A similar controversy exists concerning the *Urim* on the high priest's breastplate. Did the stones actually light up, or was the illumination confined to the prophetic consciousness of the *kohen gadol*? See my article, "The Judgement of the *Urim*", in B. Naor, *Ba-Yam Derekh* (Jerusalem, 5744).]

Whatever the case, the Maiden of Israel has been longing ever since for the pneumatic "kiss" from the Beloved's mouth: *Would that He kiss me with the kisses of His mouth!* (Song of Songs 1:2). *Face to face as on Mount Sinai* (see Rashi *ad locum*).

It is not within our power to engender authentic prophecy. That is something only the *Ribono shel 'Olam* can do. [Regarding the divine-human interaction vis-à-vis prophecy, see Maimonides, *Yad, Hil. Yesodei ha-Torah* 7:1,4-5 and *Guide*, II, 32. Also, R. A.Y. ha-Kohen Kook, *'Ittur Soferim* (Vilna, 5648/Jerusalem, 5734) I, 36-38.] This book is an attempt, spanning many years of search and meditation*, to at least come to grips in some meaningful way with a phenomenon which is most certainly at the heart of Judaism.

B.N.

Thirty-fourth day of the Omer, 5749

---

*Much of the material in Section Three was cited by me at a literary evening in Jerusalem, Adar 24, 5740. This soirée, in honor of my book, *Avirin*, was hosted by the late Prof. André (Asher Dov) Neher of Strasbourg, *zikhrono li-verakha*.

Section Four grew out of notes in my article, *Hegyonot le-Hiddush ha-Nevuah be-Yisrael* ("Thoughts for the Resumption of Prophecy in Israel"), which appeared in *Bisdeh Hemed*,

Nissan-Sivan, 5741.

At this time I should like to memorialize Rav Zevi Yehuda ha-Kohen Kook, *zekher zaddiq li-verakha,* who at a much advanced age, confided to a young man whom he just met for the first time: "I feel as if we have known each other forty years!"

1

PROPHECY/PAST

At the beginning of the Second Temple, the prophetic spirit mysteriously disappeared. Haggai, Zechariah and Malachi were the last representatives of the prophetic tradition (T.B. Sanhedrin 11a). At the same time, the Men of the Great Assembly succeeded in finally eradicating the driving compulsion for idolatry, which had plagued the Jewish People throughout the period of the First Temple and ultimately resulted in the Temple's destruction (Ibid 64a; Yoma 69b). Two unrelated events? Or perhaps some invisible thread ties them together?

1

They cried to the Lord God in a great voice (Nehemiah 9:4). What did they say? "Woe, woe. This (the evil inclination for idolatry) is what destroyed the Temple and murdered all the righteous and exiled Israel from their land, and is still taunting us. Seeing as You gave it to us only so that we might receive reward, we desire neither it, nor its reward!" A note fell from heaven on which was written: "Truth". [The signet of the Holy One is Truth. The note thus indicated divine assent.] They fasted three days and three nights. The Evil Inclination was handed over to them. It appeared as a lion of fire emerging from the site of the Holy of Holies. The prophet (Zechariah) said to Israel: "This is the Inclination for Idolatry." When they seized it, they inadvertently plucked its hair, and it let out a roar which carried four hundred parasangs. They said: "How should we act? Perhaps Heaven has had mercy on it." The prophet said to them: "Throw it in a lead pot and stop its mouth with lead, for lead absorbs sound."

Talmud Bavli, Yoma 69b; with slight variations in *Sanhedrin* 64a.

2

There is no divine spirit in the world (and therefore no prophets), for in the Second Temple the hankering for idolatry was "slaughtered". When signs were being performed by the prophets of Ba'al, if the prophets of the Lord would not have produced signs, the people would have turned to idolatry. Once the inclination to idolatry was eradicated, a prophet was no longer required.

R. Yehuda he-Hasid, *Sefer Hasidim/Book of the Pious* (Wistinetzky edition), 544.

3

Until this point there were prophets—meaning, from the time they eradicated idolatry, prophecy ceased.

Vilna Gaon, Commentary to *Seder Olam,* Chapter 30.

4

In the First Temple there were false prophets and in the Second Temple there was unfounded hatred (*Yoma* 9b).... The explanation is: Just as on the Side of Holiness there was supernatural belief, so there abounded in Israel false cults (Jeremiah 44:17-18). In the First Temple, at the peak of the Side of Holiness, the *Shekhinah* was manifest in the Holy Ark (*Yoma* 21b). On the other side, the Side of Unholiness, there arose movements inimical to belief in God: the cults of Tammuz (Ezekiel 8:14) and the Queen of Heaven (Jeremiah ibid), and false prophets (Jeremiah 27:14-15). However, in the Second Temple, where there was lacking divine manifestation (*Yoma* 21b), the Side of Unholiness was also not that powerful. Now illegitimate belief was confined to mundane matters, to believing ill about one's neighbor, when that party had in fact committed no wrong.

R. Shneur Zalman of Liady, *Liqqutey Torah* (Brooklyn, 5733)
Va'ethanan, 4c-d.

5

In every epoch, God conducts all worlds in consonance with the form Torah takes in Israel, and the nations of the world respond accordingly. The proliferation of idolatry and sorcery in the gentile world paralleled divine revelation and prophecy in Israel. When prophecy ceased and the era of the Oral Law (Talmudic dialectic) commenced, there appeared Greek Philosophy, which is to say, mortal wisdom. The Men of the Great Assembly lived at the beginning of Greek rule. That was the close of the Age of Prophecy.

R. Zadok ha-Kohen of Lublin, *Resisay Layla,* 81b.

6

"Under Hellenic domination, commenced the major thrust of Talmudic dialectic. This was initiated by Simon the Just (last of the Great Assembly), contemporary of Alexander the Great, who carried with him the seed of Greek Wisdom. In the Babylonian captivity there were yet prophets. Just as in Egyptian exile: When the time was ripe for the revelation of the Written Law, this was mirrored on the Side of Evil by the Wisdom of Egypt,

which is another way of saying Magic, a discipline found-
ed not on reason, but on forces of impurity. So too in
Babylonia, when there were still to be found among the
Men of the Great Assembly prophets—on the Other Side,
there were yet practitioners of the irrational: sorcerers,
magicians and interpreters of dreams. Later, when the
intellect of the Sages flourished into the oeuvre of the
Oral Law—on the Other Side, non-Jewish intellect mani-
fested itself in Hellenic Wisdom. The Greeks attempted
to force their system on the Jews. [In Greek Wisdom there
is a trace of good which later sages of Israel (most
prominent of whom, Maimonides) extracted. But for the
most part, the Greeks' wisdom consisted of heresy.]

R. Zadok ha-Kohen of Lublin, *Peri Zaddiq, Devarim,* 8c.

7

Intense light damages the weak-sighted. In the
spiritual realm too, in direct proportion to the intensity
of light in the generations of the prophets, was the
strength of the inclination to idolatry. The greater the
man, the greater his evil inclination. So on the national
level: in the generation of Elijah, who had sixty myriad
student-prophets, idolatry also greatly proliferated. And
when the Men of the Great Assemby eradicated the urge
for idolatry, prophecy too disappeared, for it was
necessary to dim the intensity of the light as well.

R. Zadok ha-Kohen of Lublin, *Divrei Soferim,* 21b.

8

Directly proportionate to the perfection of a human, is the imperfection . . . As it says in *Sukkah* (52a): "The greater the man, the greater his evil inclination." . . . As great as the wisdom, so is the folly great. When the light of prophecy was revealed so that one could see divine visions, there arose the evil inclination to fashion gods visible to the eye. And therefore it states in the Talmud (*Yoma* 69b), when the Men of the Great Assembly eradicated it (the inclination for idolatry), they said, "We desire neither it, nor its reward." *Its reward* refers to the perfection which resulted from it, for from the time the inclination for idolatry was uprooted, prophecy departed from Israel. Where there is no fault, there is no perfection, namely the visible "Thou"-perception of God. There remains only that form of inspiration alluded to by the Rabbis in *Bava Batra* 12a—"A sage is superior to a prophet"—as explained by Nahmanides *ad locum**.

R. Zadok ha-Kohen of Lublin, *Resisay Layla,* Chapt. 13, pp. 7b-c.

*Even though the prophecy of visionaries was taken away, the prophecy of sages, via intellect, remains and they know the truth by the divine spirit within.

Nahmanides, *Hiddushei Ramban, Bava Batra* 12a.

9

The Men of the Great Assembly mustered all their spiritual powers to eradicate from Israel the evil inclination of idolatry, in which they perceived the cause of the destruction. They were willing to sacrifice in exchange the great reward which hinged on the existence of the evil inclination and its conquest. We find in the writings of *Rabbi Zadok ha-Kohen,* of blessed memory: As long as the evil inclination existed, in opposition, prophecy and revealed miracles flourished in Israel. *One opposite the other the Lord has made* (Ecclesiastes 7:14). There is at all times a balance between the forces of holiness and impurity. As long as there was prophecy in the world, through which sensate belief was attained, there were opposing sensate forces of impurity which moved to idolatry, such as the spirit of falsehood of the prophets of Ba'al, magic, sorcery, etc. In this way free choice was preserved. And thus we see that at the beginning of the Second Temple the inclination to idolatry was purged, and correspondingly, prophecy too ceased from Israel.

R. Eliyahu E. Dessler, *Michtav me-Eliyahu,* III, 277-278.

10

In the Second Temple, when the Sages perceived the strength of the Evil Inclination, they expurgated the inclination for idolatry. The drive of this natural desire— for substantive faith—was interrupted from its healthy course, and it now functions quite lethargically. With the cessation of this intense holiness, prophecy too stopped.

R. A.Y. ha-Kohen Kook, *Ma'amrey ha-Rayah* (Jerusalem, 5744) II, 492.

11

In the world of secular knowledge, until the advent of Aristotle, inner vision dominated external rationality. Plato represents the perfection of this faculty of vision. Israelite prophecy was still vital, and its secular counterpart was of an equally visionary nature. The inclination for idolatry derived sustenance therefrom; while on the side of holiness, inner greatness of soul and sublime faith coupled with the substance of life prevailed. The cessation of prophetic inspiration in Israel, established in the secular sphere the superiority of rationality. . . . The higher conduit of Spirit was stopped up. Subsequent Greek Philosophy was unable to encompass the realm of the spirit; its doctrine of the Eternity of the World was its sore spot from a logical standpoint as well. [The appearance of Maimonides, who corrected this weakness, while at the same time being the agent for the introduction of Aristotelianism into the Camp of Israel, paved the way for supreme faith to control life's inner values.]

R. A.Y. ha-Kohen Kook, *Orot ha-Emunah*
(Jerusalem, 5745) 60.

12

Imagination no longer predominated in Israel, and the inclination for idolatry was seized in a "lead pot" and "slaughtered". By the same token, we are bereft of prophets and the flame of love for nation and land is not felt in the same profound way as in the days of old.

This is related to the pain of the world. However, at the End of Days, the traces of imagination are revealed and the love of the land is aroused. This tendency appears as yet unrefined, but it is destined to be purified. *The smallest will become a thousand, and the youngest, a powerful nation, I am the Lord, in its time I will hasten it* (Isaiah 60:22).

R. A.Y. ha-Kohen Kook, *Orot,* 36.

2

PROPHECY/PRESENT

I. THE PROPHECY OF SAGES

1

Said Rabbi Avdimi of Haifa: "Since the day the Temple was destroyed, prophecy was taken from the prophets and given to the sages." Couldn't a sage have been a prophet? This is what Rabbi Avdimi meant to say: Even though prophecy was taken from the prophets, it was not taken from the sages.

Talmud Bavli, Bava Batra 12a

2

Even though the prophecy of visionaries was taken away, the prophecy of sages, via intellect, remains and they know the truth by the divine spirit within.

Nahmanides, *Hiddushei Ramban, Bava Batra,* ibid.

3

Just as prophecy is a divine flow, so wisdom. Man cannot apprehend anything without the aid of the divine influx, as it says, *For the Lord grants wisdom* (Proverbs 2:6). This is what our Rabbis meant when they said: "Though prophecy was taken from the prophets, it was not taken from the sages" (*Bava Batra* 12a).

R. Shelomo Almoli, *Pitron ha-Halomot/Interpretation of Dreams,* 4:2.

4

It is explained in the *Pardess Rimonim* ("Orchard of Pomegranates") by R. Moshe Cordovero (*Sha'ar Mahut ve-Hanhagah,* Chapter Twenty-Six*) based on the verse (Proverbs 6:23) *Torah is light,* that in Torah too there are "residual growths" *(sefihim).* The idea is that even though we have no prophet in our midst to bestow new inspiration—no new "sowing" occurs, so to speak—nevertheless, "though prophecy was taken, it was given to the sages" (*Bava Batra* 12a). Through perseverance in Torah one can find the light of Torah, a shining light both in revealed and recondite Torah learning. Thus the metaphor (borrowed from agriculture) of "residual growths". This is the meaning of the verse (Psalms 97:11) *Light is sown for the righteous*—already sown. When there was prophecy, there was a new flow of inspiration, a revelation of light. The Rabbis said (*Hagigah* 12a): "By the light which God created the first day, Man could see from one end of the world to the other." Rejoined the Ba'al Shem Tov: "And where did He hide that light? In the Torah!" (Cf. *Tiqquney Zohar, Tiqqun* 6, "Torah is light—it is the hidden light".)

R. Menahem Mendel of Lubavitch, the *"Zemah Zedeq",*
recorded in *Siddur Maharid* (Berditchev 5673) II, 140a;
cf. opening letter in *Magen Avot* (Berditchev 5662) by
R. Shelomo Zalman of Kopust.

*See *Zohar* II, 166b and comment of R. Hayyim Vital in *Derekh Emet, ad locum.*

5

Aftergrowths of prophecies sprout forth,
and the sons of prophets awaken;
the spirit of prophecy roams the earth.

R. A.Y. ha-Kohen Kook, *Orot ha-Qodesh,* I, 157.

6

The author treats prophecy, not as a concrete corpus
of literature, but rather as a general phenomenon.
Prophecy is viewed as typical and central in Judaism.
The Holy Scriptures are viewed almost as an expression
of a spirit which pervades all paths of Judaism, rather
than a one-time happening; as a puddle flowing from
a current which permeates all Jewish existence, not as
an isolated occurrence. Bible, Halakha, Kabbala, Has-
sidism, even (granting several reservations) Medieval
Philosophy, all merge into one: Prophecy.

R. Aharon Lichtenstein in *Shivhey Qol ha-Nevuah,* 42,
evaluations of *Qol ha-Nevuah/The Voice of Prophecy,* by
R. David Cohen; appended to latter volume (Jerusalem, 5739).

7

If I were to write a "book" . . . in the "book" certainly
all must be examined in detail . . . supernal Israelite and
human thought from its very root, scaling all the world's

ideas, moving with its mighty hand all the systems and religions, their fundamentals, branches and pathways, surveying with certainty their essences and directions, and arranging them in an orderly fashion, from the bottom up, until it discovers the overall profile of man, "the Book of Man".

R. A.Y. ha-Kohen Kook, *Iggerot Rayah,* I, 50 (Letter 44).

8

Concerning the miracles performed by the *zaddiqim* (righteous) in the realm of Vienna*—they may be attributed to the fact that the followers of those *zaddiqim* are decent people who believe in them. Through the faith which they have in the words of the *zaddiq,* miracles are revealed. The *zaddiq* is certainly full of miracles, and when one believes in the *zaddiq* and focuses one's eyes and heart on his words, on each and every word, because one believes that all his words are true and righteous, and contain some meaning—the result is that afterwards when one arrives home, one examines scrupulously whatever happens, and in retrospect, understands that this was what the *zaddiq* hinted at when he spoke earlier. So the miracles were accomplished through faith. Similarly the prophets, at the time they spoke in hints, were not understood. Only later, when the prophet's words came to pass, were people able to look back and know that what he hinted at, had come about. For example, Daniel hinted the final redemption, though now the things are veiled, for one does not know how the date of redemption is alluded to in his writings. In the future,

God willing, when the predictions will be fulfilled—the
End will come and Messiah will arrive—men will in
retrospect understand how in Daniel's words was hinted
the date. The same goes for several other prophets.

R. Nahman of Bratslav, *Liqqutey Moharan,* I, 186.

*It would seem the reference is to that part of Poland which
was under Austrian rule, i.e. Galicia.

II. BAT QOL—DIVINE VOICE

1

Since the demand of the last prophets, Haggai, Zechariah and Malachi, the Holy Spirit departed from Israel. Nevertheless, they would employ the *bat qol* (divine voice).

Talmud Bavli, Sanhedrin 11a.

2

From whence do we know that we may use the *bat qol* (to decide matters)? It says (Isaiah 30:21), *Your ears shall hear the word behind you, saying.*

Talmud Bavli, Megillah 32a.

3

Said Rabbi Elazar, we may follow a *bat qol* (divine voice). Why? It says, *Your ears shall hear the word behind you, saying, 'This is the way, follow it'* (Isaiah 30:21). . . . Bar Kappara was going to a certain town. Upon arrival he hurt his finger. He then heard the voice of schoolchildren reciting the verse (Exodus 21:3), *If he entered alone, he shall leave alone.* He said, "It would seem that no other harm than this shall befall me." And so it was. Rabbi Yohanan and Rabbi Shimon ben Lakish (who lived in Israel) thought to visit Samuel (great legal authority residing in Babylonia). They said, "Let us follow a *bat qol*." They passed by the schoolhouse and heard the children recite the verse, *And Samuel died* (Samuel I 28:3), which they interpreted as a sign. Thereupon they canceled their projected journey. Later they learned that indeed Samuel had died. [However in the Babylonian Talmud's version of the story (Hullin 95b), it states that truly Samuel had not died. This was merely a heavenly ploy to spare Rabbi Yohanan the hardship of the journey.—B.N.] Rabbi Yonah and Rabbi Yosah thought to visit the ailing Rabbi Aha. They said, "Let us follow the *bat qol*." They heard a woman ask her friend, "Has the candle gone out?" She replied, "The light of Israel has not gone out, neither shall it be extinguished."

Jerusalem Talmud, Shabbat 6:9.

4

The *Zohar* (III, 169a) speaks of the Secret of the Echo *(qala de-hadra)*. . . . that which the Rabbis referred to as *bat qol* ("a *daughter* or derivative voice"). They said in the Midrash (*Shemot Rabbah*, end section 29), a human voice has a "daughter voice". See what the Tosafists (*Sanhedrin* 11a) have written concerning "since the demise of the last prophets, prophecy disappeared, but they still used the *bat qol*". The Tosafists interpret *bat qol* to be the echo of God. In *Bava Batra* (12a) the Gemara states, "prophecy was taken from prophets and given to sages", and later it states, "given to fools and children." In truth, it is all one. Our Rabbis in the Jerusalem Talmud (*Shabbat* 6:9) recount concerning the *bat qol,* that it was the voice of human beings going about their business, not intending any hidden meaning, from which the listener (who overheard the conversation) gleaned that which he needed to hear. This the Rabbis derived from the verse, *Your ears shall hear the word behind you* (Isaiah 30:21). So too in the Babylonian Talmud (*Megillah* 32a). "Behind" means that God does not relate "face to face" as He does in the case of outright prophecy. In the latter case, we know with certainty that He is giving and we are receiving. Such was prophecy: a man would recognize clearly that God was speaking to him. However, after the destruction of the Temple, the *face-à-face* perception came to a halt. There remained but the "back". The "back" refers to deeds which man has not intended. God speaks through these people who intend something totally different. This is the Divine Echo. Natural science informs us that an echo is created when sound strikes against some hard substance. The scientists construct towers in which sound echoes over and over several times, as related in their books. The echo sounds as if it is an independent voice, but it is only the "back" of the original voice.

All men's actions and talk are from God, that which God does and speaks at a given moment. However, as it says, *God gives one word which is broadcast to a mighty host* (Psalms 68:12). God's speech spreads in several directions, echoing through each creature's receptacle. (The tone an echo takes, depends on the hardness and texture of the substance it encounters.) All human speech is but the echo of God. For example, when God speaks good, then all creations want good and speak of it, but each one according to its conception of good. Thus Jews speak of what good represents to them and non-Jews of what it means to them, each nation according to its character. To one nation, good is synonymous with wealth; to another, it signifies sexual license; to yet another, murder, or empire, etc. The same applies to animals according to their characteristics. This is in general. So too on the individual level. Thus, it becomes utterly impossible to discern the true Voice of God and His will, since there has been imposed on it the human intellect, and the Voice has become multifarious. [It may be discerned only by those who employ the *bat qol*. As mentioned above, sometimes one senses clearly that this is the Echo of God. The *Gemara Megillah* 32a gives the examples of a man's voice heard in the home, or a women's voice sensed in the field. (These are infrequent occurrences.) It further stipulates that the same sound be heard twice.] Now prophecy belongs to fools and children who do not yet have independent thought; their voice is the "back" of the voice of God, the Divine Echo. [Fools and children are simple vessels in whom the echo is undisturbed by thought and is therefore clear.]

And so does prophecy belong to sages, meaning the true Sages of Israel who recognize that all their wisdom is from God. Nevertheless, it is not really face-à-face, as was the case with the prophets who could state "thus saith the Lord", because their wisdom did not issue at all from themselves. The wisdom of the Sages of Israel flows from their own hearts, but is the echo of God's voice. The voice of wisdom is conceived through the voice of God. It appears as if it were the sage's own voice, but actually it is but the voice of God—not the "front", but the "back" resounding from the human heart, appearing to be original. [The Oral Law is the echo of the Written Law. And the echo of the *Mishnah* subsequently produced the echo of the *Gemara*. And the echo of the Sages of the Talmud gave vent to the echo of the Later Sages. And all are but extensions of the Voice of the Lord contained in the Written Law. The echo rebounds several times as in nature.]

R. Zadok ha-Kohen of Lublin, *Dover Zedeq,* 71d-72c.

5

All of this world is a clothing of the lower levels of holiness, the "feet" of holiness, as it says, *the earth is My footstool* (Isaiah 66:1). . . . Every day there is thought, speech and action, and God constricts His divinity from infinity to the finitude of the corporeal world, and sends each man thought, speech and action, according to the day, the man and the place, and encloses therein hints to beckon him to His service. So one must meditate on this, to understand specifically what these hints mean, whether it be work or trade, etc.

R. Nahman of Bratslav, *Liqqutey Moharan* I, 54:2.

3

PROPHECY/FUTURE

Man is free in his imagination and a prisoner of his intellect.

—R. ISRAEL SALANTER, *IGGERET HA-MUSSAR*

1

Know that true prophecy essentially is the flow which descends from God. . . . on the intellect first, and after on the imagination. Prophecy is the highest human level, the most perfection which may be found in humankind. It involves the perfection of the imaginative faculty. Not all men are capable of prophecy. It is not something which might be attained merely by immersion in analytical studies or ethical self-improvement. There must be added to them the perfection of the imaginative faculty at birth, as much as is possible.

Maimonides, *Guide of the Perplexed* II, 36.

2

The intellectual influx, flowing on the rational faculty alone, and not on the imaginative faculty—this is the condition of *the class of men of science engaged in philosophical speculation.* On the other hand, the influx impinging on both the rational and imaginative faculties—is characteristic of the *class of the prophets.* And again, the flow reaching the imaginative faculty alone, while the rational is deficient—characterizes the *class of politicians, legislators, magicians, soothsayers, clairvoyants, and wonder-workers.* Seeing as they are not men of science, they all belong to the third class. [Italics mine—B.N.]

Maimonides, *Guide* II, 37.

3

You know that any physical power becomes weakened and attenuated at times, and strengthened at others. This imaginative faculty is indubitably a physical power. Therefore you will find that the prophets lose their prophetic ability at times of mourning or anger and the like. The Rabbis said: "Prophecy rests neither through sadness nor lassitude." In addition, they said that Jacob our Father did not prophesy during his period of mourning, as his imagination was consumed with the disappearance of Joseph. They said too, that Moses our Master, of blessed memory, did not prophesy (as before) after the murmuring of the Spies, until all the generation of the desert had died, as their incessant complaining fatigued him. . . . Furthermore, you will find that some prophets prophesied for a while and then desisted, on account of some development which occurred. This is undoubtedly the essential and proximate cause for the cessation of prophecy in the time of Exile: the lassitude or morbidity which a man suffers for various reasons, worst of which is his being a slave to the ignorant who combine the privation of reason and the height of bestiality—while he is powerless against them. Concerning this it was bleakly prophesied: *They will cast about to seek the word of God and will not find* (Amos 8:12); *Her king and officers among the nations, there is no Torah, neither did her prophets find a vision of God* (Lamentations 2:9). Verily the reason is apparent: the vessel (i.e. the imaginative faculty) has ceased to function. And this (i.e. resumption of imagination) too will be the cause for the return of prophecy to us as before, as promised in the days of Messiah, may he be revealed soon.

Maimonides, *Guide* II, 36.

4

Know that there is a Light which is above *nefesh-ruah-neshama* (three levels of soul), and it is the Light of *En Sof* (the Infinite). Even though the mind cannot grasp the Light, thought pursues it. And through this pursuit, the mind grasps the Light in the manner of *maté-we'lo-maté* ("arrives, but does not arrive"). For truly the mind cannot grasp *En Sof*, it is beyond *nefesh-ruah-neshama* (three levels of soul). . . .

If one has perfected the Harmonizer and Organizer (i.e. the harmonizing and organizing faculty), which we refer to as *Keter* ("Crown"), what transpires when the mind pursues the light of *En Sof* (the Infinite), is that the *Keter* ("Crown") holds back the mind, in order to harmonize the mind. The consciousness, on the other hand, bombards the Harmonizer and Organizer. And through this tug-of-war of pursuit and restraint are created Palaces for the Light of the Infinite *(hekhalin le-or En Sof)*. . . .

[The Crown is what balances and orders the mind. It is the ability of man's mind to balance and order consciousness so that it does not overstep the bounds. This faculty is like a partition between the brain and the Infinite Light. . . . Through pursuit and restraint—the pursuit of the Infinite by the mind, and the restraining action of the Harmonizer and Organizer, i.e. *Keter* ("Crown")—through both of these aspects, the consciousness bombards the "partition", and thereby are created "Palaces of the Infinite Light". This means that vessels and palaces are created of the highest spirituality, in order to thereby grasp *En Sof*, blessed be He, in the manner of *maté-we'lo-maté* ("arrives but does not arrive"). For if there would not be something to hold back the mind from its relentless pursuit, the mind would be totally obliterated and man would cease to exist, for the light of *En Sof* cannot be grasped.]

R. Nahman of Bratslav, *Liqqutey Moharan* I, 24.

5

Truly Jews are far from idolatry, for Jews represent the light of true holy intellect, and the idolaters represent the imaginative faculty. In man there is intellect and imagination. The imaginative faculty is also a faculty of the mind, a lower faculty which imagines and portrays in the mind all things physical, bringing them all to mind. And one who has true reason, must assert reason over imagination, by divesting everything of its corporeality. One should comprehend thereby the greatness of God, until the thought be divested of its corporeality, which is imagination, and return to reason to be consumed in *En Sof*, the Creator, blessed be He. For this is the essence of reason: to recognize God, to overcome the imaginative faculty which is clothed in the corporeality of creation, and to ascend to true intellectual apprehension; to recognize the Creator Who is above all the pictures and icons of the imaginative faculty, for all pictures and images draw from the Infinite One, Who is without form.

R. Nathan Sternharz of Nemirov (disciple of R. Nahman of Bratslav), *Liqqutey Halakhot, Hilkhot 'Avodat Elilim* 3:2.

6

The spirit will flow on all humans through the prophetic and visionary influence of Israel, which is dependent on the holiness of the "hips", of *Nezah* and *Hod* (literally "Endurance" and "Splendor", names of two *sefirot* symbolized bt the two hips), for from there emanates the inspiration of the prophets. . . . Prophecy is possible only through the perfection of *qedushat ha-berit* (holiness in the sexual sphere), which is the holiness of the hips.

R. Zadok ha-Kohen of Lublin, *Poqed 'Aqarim,* 14d.

7

[Beshtian] Hasidism turned to feeling and imagination more than to reason and action, and for this reason stepped up the demand for fleshly purity *(miqweh)*.

R. A.Y. ha-Kohen Kook, *Orot,* 81.

8

If the New Science brags that it has been liberated from Theology, it must know that by the same token, Theology has been freed of Science, which bound her in human chains. However, certainly a new name is required for the sublime subject, not a name coined by

men, but a new name given by God. Theology freed of
the fetters of Science, is *Prophecy,* the treasure of Israel,
which will be revealed to us soon.

R. A.Y. ha-Kohen Kook, *'Arpiley Tohar* (Jerusalem, 5743) 40.

9

All of contemporary society is built on the foundation
of the imaginative faculty. This is the pagan legacy of
the nations caught up in the imaginative faculty, from
which developed esthetics, both live and plastic. The
imaginative faculty progresses, and with it the applied
and empirical sciences, and in proportion to the
ascendence of the imaginative faculty, the light of
intellect recedes, because the entire world supposes that
all happiness depends on the development of the
imaginative faculty. So things continue gradually, until
the remains of reason in the spirit of secular wisdom
are also converted to the imaginative faculty. The
novelists and raconteurs, the dramaturges and all engaged in *les beaux arts,* assume prominence in society,
while philosophy hobbles and totters, because pure
reason disappears. As much as reason recedes, so *im-
pudence increases, and the wisdom of sages "rots", the
sin-fearing are reviled and truth is absent, and the face
of the generation is as the face of a dog (Sotah* 49b). . . .
But all of this is a far-reaching plan, God's plan to
perfect the imaginative faculty, for imagination is the
healthy basis for the supernal spirit which will descend
on it. [As a result of the dominance of the spiritual (intellectual?) perception which preceded in Israel, the

imaginative faculty was forced to collapse, weakening the position of supernal divine spirit destined to come through King Messiah.] Therefore, now the imaginative faculty is being firmly established. When it will be finished, the throne will be ready and complete for the supernal spirit of God, fit to receive the light of the divine spirit, which is the spirit of God, *a spirit of wisdom and understanding, a spirit of counsel and strength, knowledge and fear of God* (Isaiah 11:2).

R. A.Y. ha-Kohen Kook, *Orot*, 34-35.

10

How is it possible to be cured of those delusions (engendered by ego)? Regarding this question too, Hasidism gives a most simple solution: by other images which are true. It would be proper for us to become accustomed already in our youth to working with the imaginative ability which is in us, to develop and perfect it, in order to enable us to picture in our minds true images, so as to gradually weaken the vain delusions within and be cured of them. . . .

To begin, we shall explain the imagination which illumines us and opens our eyes to see our true situation and value in the world and our terrible lowliness. In order to reach this, one should commence thus: First we shall attempt to picture in our minds by means of the imaginative ability within us, the planet Earth. We shall imagine that we see from afar the entire globe with its continents and all the seas which encircle them. We should picture too all the nations which inhabit the continents, according to their languages and borders, and the total population of each nation and tongue. All this we should picture vividly, as if seeing this vista right before us with our corporeal sense of vision. Initially this imaging will not affect us much, for it is as yet novel. Our imagination is yet weak, for we have not yet made much use of it, but gradually, if we apply ourselves and exercise daily (and when possible, several times a day), we shall behold this, with our spiritual eyes and our minds' eyes, with increasing clarity and vividness, as if it were possible to touch this vision with the hands.

We should imagine not only people, but also the other creations found in the world: All the animals and beasts with which we are acquainted, where they are found, their appearances and natures—the multitude of predators in the deserts and forests; the domestic animals, how men use them and benefit from them; other tiny creatures, such as flies, and those large, such as elephants; serpents and reptiles, how they creep, run, rest, eat, are born and die. All the species of birds, the endless variations of chirping and singing, sung in air, in trees, in fields and vineyards. The multitude of fish in seas and rivers, how they swim, are swallowed, born, captured and die. All the species of plants, grains, vegetables, grasses, thorns, flowers, gardens, orchards, fields, vineyards and forests. All those as we know them: their appearance, how they grow, develop, mature, dry, wither and fall. All this we should picture in great detail and specificity, and again as a whole, as we know them, either directly or through reading and education.

After a certain amount of time—depending on individual nature and assiduity—this project will become quite clear, we will see these scenes with great clarity, until we are affected and feel how this great vision influences and charms us, like the man who has been moved by the beauty of nature which he sees with his physical eyes. Then we shall proceed further and attempt to picture the place where *we* are now standing, and try to present ourselves among all those people and creations. At first it will be exceedingly difficult to picture this, for the ego and self-importance so deeply ingrained in us, will resist and not allow us in any way to become lost and submerged in the crowd of all those creatures, will not allow us to sacrifice our imaginary grandeur, and see the not so pleasant truth, which is our terrible lowliness and smallness. However, habit will do its part; eventually we will succeed in overcoming all blocks, and it shall become increasingly easy to picture with our gift of imagination this marvelous vision.

R. Menahem Eckstein, *Tena'ey ha-Nefesh le-Hassagat ha-Hasidut/Conditions of the Soul for Attainment of Hasidut* (Vienna, 5621) 2-4.

4

VISIONARY COSMOLOGIES

I. EZEKIEL'S VISION

And I saw, and behold, a storm-wind came out of the north, a great cloud, and a flaming fire, and a brightness was on it round about; and out of the midst of it was like the glitter of electrum, out of the midst of the fire. And out of the midst thereof, I saw the likeness of four living creatures. And this was their appearance: They had the likeness of a man, and every one had four faces, and every one of them had four wings.

Ezekiel 1:4-6.

And four faces to each, and four faces to each of those; sixteen faces per creature; the number of faces of the four creatures equaling sixty-four, and four wings to each, and four to each of those; sixteen wings to each face; sixty-four wings per creature, totalling two hundred and fifty-six wings for the four creatures.

Targum, ibid, verse 6.

And every one had four faces—the face of man had four faces, and so the lion and the eagle and the ox—sixteen per creature. And four wings to each face—sixty-four wings per creature.

Rashi, ibid.

It is quite apparent that in Ezekiel's vision, known as *Ma'aseh Merkavah* ("Work of the Chariot"), we have a geometric or exponential progression: 4 x 4 x 4 x 4. Is this perhaps a mathematical expression for a taste of infinity?

II. SOURCE FOR SYMBOLS AND THEORIES OF ARI (R. ISAAC LURIA)— "ECSTATIC EXPERIENCE"

According to R. Moshe Hayyim Luzzato, *Zimzum* ("Cosmic Contraction") was seen in a vision. Just as in the Work of the Chariot, there is vision and interpretation, sight and understanding.

R. David Cohen, *Qol ha-Nevuah/The Voice of Prophecy,* 213, citing R. Moshe Hayyim Luzzato, *Qalah Pitehey Hokhmah/ One Hundred Thirty-Eight Doors of Wisdom,* door xxiv, *zimzum,* commentary.

All this *[Zimzum]* is similar to the visions of Isaiah and Ezekiel, the so-called Work of the Chariot. One sees its order and comprehends thereby the magnitude of the Lord's orchestration.

R. Moshe Hayyim Luzzato, *Commentary to Ozerot Hayyim,*1, (cf. 18), printed in *Ginzei RaMHaL,* (B'nei Beraq, 5740) 297.

This is not the way the Ari [R. Isaac Luria] of blessed

memory, arrived at those notions. It is a known fact that he did not concoct metaphors to garb his concepts, for if so, why choose these (strange) metaphors? Also, certainly an enormous amount of time is required to fit the symbols to the concepts. In truth, all of his conceptions had their source in vision. He saw this entire panorama the way Ezekiel saw [the Work of] the Chariot.

R. Zadok ha-Kohen of Lublin, *Sefer ha-Zikhronot* (appended to *Divrei Soferim*) 31b.

III. MATHEMATICAL THEORIES OF R. SHEMTOV GEFFEN ORIGINATED WITH VISION

Suddenly there appeared before my aching eyes some great light, and infinite dimensions stood before my mind's eye, while my eyes of flesh were closed. It seemed to me as if I truly experienced the many dimensions with my senses—once and never again—and I walked in their midst.

ShemTov Geffen, *Memadim-Nevuah-Admatanut/Dimensions-Prophecy-Geology* (Jerusalem, 5734) 27-28, "Memoirs".

אורות הנבואה

בצלאל נאור

חלק עברי

א

הנבואה / עבר

בתחילת בית שני נסתלקה השראת הנבואה. חגי, זכריה
ומלאכי היו הנביאים האחרונים (סנהדרין יא,א). בעת ובעונה אחת,
הצליחו אנשי כנסת הגדולה לבטל היצר לעבודה זרה, מה שהיה
בעוכרם של ישראל רוב ימי בית ראשון, ושגרם לחורבנו. שתי עובדות
בלתי־קשורות? או שמא איזה חוט בלתי־נראה מקשר אותן?

1

ויצעקו אל ה' אלקים בקול גדול (נחמיה ט,ד). מאי אמור?
בייא, בייא, היינו האי דאחרביה למקדשא, וקליה להיכלא,
וקטלינהו לכולהו צדיקי, ואגלינהו לישראל מארעהון, ועדיין
מרקד בינן. כלום יהבתיה לן אלא לקבולי ביה אגרא?! לא איהו
בעינן ולא אגריה בעינן! נפל להו פיתקא מרקיעא דהוה כתב ביה
אמת. אותיבו בתעניתא תלתא יומין ותלתא לילואתא. מסרוה
ניהליהו. נפק אתא כי גוריא דנורא מבית קדש־הקדשים. אמר להו
נביא לישראל, היינו יצרא דעבודה זרה. בהדי דתפסוה ליה
אשתמיט ביניתא ממזייא ורמא קלא ואזל קליה ארבע מאה
פרסי. אמרו, היכי נעביד, דילמא חס ושלום מרחמי עליה מן
שמיא? אמר להו נביא, שדיוהו בדודא דאברא, וחפיוהו לפומיה
באברא, דאברא משאב שאיב קלא.

1

[וַיִּזְעֲקוּ אֶל ה' אֱלֹקִים בְּקוֹל גָּדוֹל (נחמיה ט,ד). מה אמרו? וי, וי, זה הוא שהחריב את בית-המקדש, ושרף היכלו, והרג את כל הצדיקים, והגלה את ישראל מארצם, ועדיין מרקד ביננו. כלום נתתו לנו אלא לקבל עליו שכר? איננו רוצים לא אותו ולא שכרו. נפל להם פתק מן השמים שהיה כתוב בו "אמת" [חותמו של הקדוש-ברוך-הוא אמת, "כלומר מסכים אני עמכם" (רש"י)]. ישבו בתענית שלושה ימים ושלושה לילות. הופיע כגור-אריה של אש יוצא מבית קדש-הקדשים. אמר להם נביא [רש"י: "זכריה בן עדו"] לישראל, זהו יצר עבודה-זרה. כאשר תפסו אותו נתלש ממנו שער, והרים קולו, והלך הקול ארבע מאות פרסה. אמרו, איך נעשה? שמא, חס ושלום, מרחמים עליו מן השמים. אמר להם הנביא, זרקוהו בסיר של עופרת, וסתמו פיו בעופרת, שעופרת בולעת הקול.]

יומא סט,ב, ובשינויים קלים בסנהדרין סד,א.

2

וְאֵין רוּחַ הַקּוֹדֶשׁ בָּעוֹלָם לִהְיוֹת נְבִיאִים בָּעוֹלָם בְּבַיִת שֵׁנִי, מִפְּנֵי שֶׁבַּבַּיִת שֵׁנִי נִשְׁחַט יֵצֶר עֲבוֹדָה זָרָה, וּכְשֶׁהָיוּ אוֹתָן נְבִיאֵי הַבַּעַל, אִם לֹא הָיוּ נְבִיאֵי ה' עוֹשִׂים, הָיוּ נֶהְפָּכִים לַעֲבוֹדָה זָרָה, וּכְשֶׁנִּשְׁחַט יֵצֶר הָרַע שֶׁל עֲבוֹדָה זָרָה, כְּבָר לֹא הָיוּ צְרִיכִים לִנְבִיא.

ספר חסידים (מהדורת ויסטינצקי) תקמד.

3

עַד כָּאן הָיוּ הַנְּבִיאִים — פֵּירוּשׁ, מִשֶּׁהָרְגוּ אֶת הַיֵּצֶר הָרַע, בָּטְלָה הַנְּבוּאָה.

פירוש הגר"א לסדר עולם, פרק ל.

4

בית ראשון היו בו נביאי השקר ובית שני היה בו שנאת חנם
. . . והענין, כי כמו שיש בסטרא דקדושה בחינת אמונה שהיא
למעלה מן הדעת, כך היו אז בין ישראל אמונות כוזבות (כמבואר
בירמיהו מד,יז-יח). והם זה לעומת זה. והנה בבית ראשון
בהתגברות סטרא דקדושה היה גילוי שכינה, ארון וכפורת, וכך
בזה לעומת זה, בהתגברות סטרא דקליפה מחמת החטא היה
התגברות כנגד אמונת אלקות, והנשים שהיו מבכות את התמוז
(יחזקאל ח,יד) אמרו מעת חדלנו לקטר למלכת השמים חסרנו וגו'
(ירמיהו שם), וכך היו נביאי השקר (כמ"ש בירמיה כז,יד-טו),
דהיינו אמונות כוזבות בנביא להאמין במה שלא דבר ה'. מה
שאין כן בבית שני שחסרו חמשה דברים לא היתה גם כן בלעומת
זה התגברות הקליפה כל כך והיתה האמונה רעה במילי דעלמא
להאמין באנשי רכיל לשנוא את חבירו, שהשנאה ההיא היא
שנאת חנם שחבירו לא עשה לו רעה באמת.

ר' שניאור זלמן מלאדי, לקוטי תורה (ברוקלין, תשל"ג) ואתחנן, ד, ג-ד.

5

ולעולם כפי הנהגת התורה בישראל, כן היא הנהגתו יתברך
כל העולמות, ואף האומות מתנהגים כן ב"זה לעומת זה". וכל
ריבוי עבודה-זרה אצלם וחרטומים ומכשפים היה כל זמן שהיה
גילוי שכינה ונבואה בישראל, ומשנסתלקה והתחיל תורה שבעל-
פה, התחיל גם כן אצלם חכמת יוונית, שהיא חכמה אנושית. כי
התחלת אנשי כנסת הגדולה היתה בתחלת מלכות יוון, שאז היתה
חתימת הנבואה.

ר' צדוק הכהן מלובלין, רסיסי לילה, פא,ב.

6

ב[גלות] יון התחיל עיקר התפשטות פלפול תורה שבעל־פה על־ידי שמעון הצדיק, שהיה משיירי כנסת הגדולה, ואז בזמנו היה אלכסנדרוס מוקדון, והתחיל אז חכמת יוונית. שבבבל היו עדיין נביאים. וכמו במצרים, שהיה אז הזמן להתגלות תורה שבכתב, היה לעומת זה בקליפה חכמת מצרים, שהיה עיקרם כישוף וכדומה שאינו על־פי שכל, רק מכוחות הטומאה. וכן בבבל, שהיו באנשי כנסת הגדולה עוד נביאים אחרונים, היו לעומת זה עוד חרטומים ואשפים ופותרי חלומות, שלא על־פי שכל, רק בכוחות הטומאה. ואחר כך כשהתחיל עיקר התפשטות תורה שבעל־פה משכל החכמים שהופיע עליהם, אז התחיל לעומת זה חכמת יוונית, שהיתה גם כן על־פי שכל שלהם. והם רצו להכניס מינות וחכמת (!) שלהם חס ושלום בישראל. ובחכמת יוונית היה בו כן כן ניצוץ מועט מהטוב שמזה הוציאו מהם הרמב״ם וכדומה מחכמי ישראל. אך עיקר חכמתם היה מינות ורצו להכניס זאת בישראל חס ושלום.

ר' **צדוק הכהן מלובלין**, פרי צדיק, דברים, ח,ג.

7

ריבוי האור מזיק לחלושי הראות, וברוחניות גם־כן כפי ריבוי האור שהיה בדורות הנביאים, כן זה־לעומת־זה גבר אז יצרא דעבודה זרה, דכל הגדול מחבירו, יצרו גדול, וכן בכלל האומה, ובדור אליהו שהיו לו יותר משישים רבוא נביאים תלמידים, היה ריבוי עבודה זרה גם־כן, ואנשי כנסת הגדולה שבטלו יצרא דעבודה זרה, אז נסתלקה גם־כן הנבואה, כי הוצרך להעלים הבהירות גם־כן.

ר' **צדוק הכהן מלובלין**, דברי סופרים, כא,ב.

8

כפי המעלה והשלימות שיש לאדם, כך יש לעומתו חסרון
כנגדו ממש כפי ערכו . . . והוא כדרך שכתוב בסוכה (נב,א) כל
הגדול מחבירו, יצרו גדול הימנו . . . וכפי גדלות החכמה, כך יש
גדלות שטות. ובהיות יצרא דעבודה־זרה שליט, היינו להיות אור
הנבואה נגלה אז להיות רואה בעין מראות אלהים, מזה נמשך
יצר הרע לעשות אלהים אחרים הנגלים לעין, ולכן אמרו ביומא
(סט,ב) דכשבטלוהו אנשי כנסת הגדולה, אמרו, לא איהו בעינו
ולא אגריה (=לא אותו אנו רוצים, ולא שכרו) , פירוש אגריה
(=שכרו), השלימות הנמשך ממנו, כי מעת שנעקר יצרא דעבודה־
זרה, נסתלקה נבואה מישראל. כי כאשר אין חסרון בזה, אין
שלימות, להיות הכרת הנוכח דאלקי אמת לעין, רק בהעלם,
כטעם חכם עדיף מנביא, שהוא על־ידי רוח הקודש, עיין שם
ברמב"ן בבבא בתרא (יב,א) [ראה למטה], והוא מצד ההעלם.

ר' צדוק הכהן מלובלין, רסיסי לילה (סימן יג) ז,ב־ג.

אעפ"י שנטלה נבואת הנביאים שהוא המראה והחזון,
נבואת החכמים שהיא בדרך החכמה לא נטלה, אלא יודעים
האמת ברוח הקודש שבקרבם.

חידושי הרמב"ן, בבא בתרא יב,א.

9

ראו אנשי כנסת הגדולה צורך להשתדל בכל כחותיהם
הרוחניים לבטל מישראל את יצר הרע של עבודה זרה, שבו ראו
סיבת החורבן. והיו מוכנים לוותר תמורת זה על השכר הגדול
הכרוך במציאות יצר הרע הזה וכיבושו. ומצינו בדברי ר' צדוק
הכהן זצ"ל, שכל עוד שהיה קיים יצר הרע של עבודה זרה, היתה
כנגדו הנבואה והיו נסים גלויים בישראל. כי זה לעומת זה עשה
האלקים, שכן לעולם יש שיווי משקל בין כחות הקדושה

והטומאה, וכל זמן שהיתה נבואה בעולם שעל ידה משיגים אמונה חושית, היו לעומתה גם כחות טומאה מוחשיים שפעלו לצד העבודה־זרה, כגון רוח שקר של נביאי הבעל, כישוף, קסם וכו', וזה כדי שתישאר בחירה חפשית. וכן רואים אנו שבתחלת ימי בית השני בטל יצרא דעבודה זרה, ולעומתו פסקה גם הנבואה מישראל.

רא"א דסלר, מכתב מאליהו, ג, 277־278.

10

בבית שני, כשראו חכמינו את תוקף יצר הרע, בטלוהו ליצרא דעבודה זרה. שאת התשוקה הטבעית הזאת — לתוכן אמוני — הפסיקו ממהלכה הבריא, והנהו מתנהג ברפיון ובכבדות, ועם בהירות הקודש שנפסקה, חדלה אז גם נבואה מישראל.

ראי"ה קוק, מאמרי הראי"ה ב' (ירוש' ה'תשד"ם) עמ' 492.

11

בחכמת העולם, עד השפעתו של אריסטו, היתה החזיוניות הפנימית מתגברת יותר מהתכונה המושכלת על־פי הערכים החיצונים, שהעלה אפלטון את התכונה ההיא לצורה משוכללת. אותו הליח של הנבואה שבישראל עדיין היה קיים, וכעין טיבו היתה התיצרותה של בינת האדם החילונית. בנטיית הצדדים היה יצרא דעבודה זרה מתפרנס ממנה, ובקדושה, גדולת הנשמה בפנימיותה, ושיגוב האמונה בתוכן החיים. הפסקת רוח הקודש הנבואית מישראל בססה בצורה החלונית את המעמד של התגברותה של הרציונליות . . . נסתם השביל העליון אשר למהלך הרוח. לא יכלה החכמה היוונית המאוחרת להתפשט על כל המילוי הרוחני, יסוד קדמות העולם שלה הונח ברפיון גם מצד המשקל ההגיוני. והופעתו של הרמב"ם לברר תוכן חולשה זו, בעת

שעל ידו באה השפעה אריסטוקרטית לתוך מחנה ישראל, היא דוקא פלסה את הנתיב לערך האמונה היותר עליון לשלוט על כל ערכי החיים הפנימיים.

רא"יה קוק, אורות האמונה (ירוש' תשמ"ה) עמ' 60.

12

נתגרש כח המדמה משליטה רחבה בגבול ישראל, וייצרא דעבודה-זרה נעצר ב"דודא דאברא" (=בדוד אבר) "ונכיס יצרא" (=ונשחט היצר), ולעומת זה אין עוד נביא ולהבת אהבת האומה והארץ איננה מורגשת באותו הטעם העמוק של ימי הטובה. והדברים מקושרים עם צער העולם כולו, עד שבאחרית הימים עקבות כח המדמה מתגלים ואהבת הארץ מתעוררת. מתראה הדבר בשמריו, אבל עומד הוא להזדכך. "הקטן יהיה לאלף והצעיר לגוי עצום, אני ד' בעתה אחישנה".

רא"יה קוק, אורות, עמ' לו.

ב

הנבואה / הוה

א) נבואת חכמים

1

אמר רבי אבדימי דמן חיפא, מיום שחרב בית־המקדש, ניטלה נבואה מן הנביאים וניתנה לחכמים. אטו חכם לאו נביא הוא? הכי קאמר, אף על־פי שניטלה מן הנביאים, מן החכמים לא ניטלה.

בבא בתרא יב,א.

אטו חכם לאו נביא הוא. וכי אין חכם ראוי להיות נביא, דקאמר מר ניטלה מן הנביאים ונתנה לחכמים, מכלל דמעיקרא לא היתה נבואה לחכמים. הכי קאמר אף על־פי שניטלה מן הנביאים. שאינם חכמים, מן חכמים לא ניטלה.

רש"י שם.

8

2

אעפ"י שנטלה נבואת הנביאים שהוא המראה והחזון, נבואת החכמים שהיא בדרך החכמה לא נטלה, אלא יודעים האמת ברוח הקודש שבקרבם.

חידושי הרמב"ן שם.

3

כשם שהנבואה היא שפע אלקות, כן החכמה, וזה שהאדם אינו משיג שום מושכל מעצמו אם לא יסייע לו השפע האלקי, כמו שאמר הכתוב (משלי ב,ו) כי ה' יתן חכמה וגו', וזה שאמרו רבותינו ז"ל אף על-פי שניטלה נבואה מן הנביאים, מן החכמים לא ניטלה.

ר' שלמה אלמולי, פתרון החלומות, שער ד, פרק ב.

4

הנה מבואר בפרדס, סוף שער מהות והנהגה, פרק כו [ראה זוהר, תרומה קסו,ב ופירוש "דרך אמת" לר' חיים ויטאל שם — ב.נ.] והנה כתיב (משלי ו,כג) ותורה אור, שבתורה יש בה גם-כן ספיחים. ורוצה לומר, כי אף שאין אתנו נביא, שהוא השפעה חדשה ע"י גננא בגנתא (="גנן בגן") זריעה חדשה, מכל מקום אף שניטלה נבואה, נתנה לחכמים (בבא בתרא יב,א) שעל-ידי עמל תורה יוכל למצוא אור תורה, אור המאיר, הן בנגלה והן בנסתר, פנימיות התורה. וזהו כעניין הספיחים, והיינו אור זרוע, אור התורה זרוע כבר כו'. מה שאין כן כשהיתה נבואה, היתה זו נביעה חדשה, גילוי אור כו'. וזה שאמרו רבותינו, זכרונם לברכה (חגיגה יב,א) אור שנברא ביום ראשון היה מביט בו מסוף העולם ועד סופו כו'. "והיכן גנזו? — גנזו בתורה" (המאמר ידוע מהבעש"ט

נ"ע זיע"א, ועיין בתקוני זוהר, תיקונא שתיתאה, ותורה אור —
ואיהו אור הגנוז).

ר' מנחם מענדל מליובאוויץ', בעל "צמח צדק", הובא בסידור הרב מלאדי עם
פירוש מהרי"ד (ברדיצ'ב, תרע"ג) חלק שני, קמ,א, ענין נסיעות והשתטחות,
וכעין זה באגרת רש"ז מקאפוסט שנדפסה בתחילת ספרו "מגן אבות"
(ברדיצ'ב, תרס"ב).

5

ספיחי נבואות הנה צומחים,
ובני נביאים מתעוררים,
רוח הנבואה הולך ושט בארץ . . .

ראי"ה קוק, אורות הקודש, א, קנז.

6

המחבר אינו דן בנבואה כחליפת כתבים וספרים מגובשת,
אלא כתופעה כללית. הנבואה נראית כטיפוסית וכמרכזית
ביהדות. אדרבה, כתבי־הקודש כמעט שנראים כביטוי לרוח
השוררת בכל שבילי היהדות, לא כתופעה חד־פעמית; כשלולית
הנובעת מזרם השוטף בכל מציאות כנסת־ישראל, לא כמקרה
בודד. נ"ך, הלכה, קבלה, חסידות, אפילו (אם כי בצירוף כמה
הסתייגויות) פילוסופיית ימי הביניים — הכל עולה בקנה אחד —
קנה הנבואה.

ר' אהרן ליכטנשטיין, ב"שבחי קול הנבואה", עמ' מב, נספח ל־קול הנבואה,
ר' דוד כהן (ירוש' תשל"ט).

7

אילו כתבתי "ספר" . . . ב"ספר" ודאי צריך לברר את הכל בפרטיות . . . על־עליונות המחשבה הישראלית והאנושית משורש שרשה, המטפסת על־גבי כל הרעיונות העולמיים, המניעה בחוזק ידה את כל השיטות והדתות, בעקריהן, שרשיהן סעיפיהן וארחותיהן, וסוקרת בבטחה על תמציתן ומגמת פניהן, ומערכת אותן כולן במערכה סידורית, ממטה למעלה, עד שהיא מוצאת את הפרצוף האנושי הכללי, "ספרא דאדם".

ראי"ה קוק, אגרות הראיה א, נ (אג' מד).

8

מה שמספרים מופתים מהצדיקים שבמדינות קיר"ה (=קיסר, ירום הודו) דוויין (=בירת אוסטריה). הוא מחמת שאנשיהם הם אנשים כשרים ומאמינים בהצדיקים, כי על־ידי אמונה שהם מאמינים בדברי הצדיק, על־ידי זה מתגלים מופתים, כי באמת הצדיק בודאי מלא מופתים, וכשהוא מאמין בהצדיק ונותן עיניו ולבו על דברי הצדיק. על כל דיבור ודיבור, כי מאמין שכל דבריו אמת וצדק, ובכוונה מכוונת אזי אחר־כך כשבא לביתו, כל מה שיארע אותו, הוא מסתכל היטב על כל דבר שיארע לו, ומבין למפרע בדברי הצדיק שדיבר עמו בהיותו אצלו, שזה היתה כוונת הצדיק שרמז לו בתוך דברים שדיבר עמו, וכן כל דבר ודבר שיזדמן לו, הוא מוצא הכל בדברי הצדיק למפרע, שרמז לו שיהיה כן, נמצא שנעשו ונתגלו המופתים על־ידי זה, וכן מצינו אצל הנביאים שבעת שאמר הנביא הנבואה היתה ברמז, ולא היו מבינים נבואתו בפירוש על מה מרמז, ואחר־כך כשנתקיימו דברי הנביא , היו יודעין למפרע שנתקיימו דברי הנביא שהתנבא ורמז על זה מקודם, והבינו דברי הנביא למפרע שהתכוון על זה, וכמו שמצינו בדניאל שמרמז על סוף קץ הגאולה, ועתה הדברים סתומים, כמו שכתוב שם (יב,ד) סתום הדברים וחתום, כי אין אדם יודע עתה איך מרומז שם זמן הגאולה, אבל לעתיד, אם ירצה

השם, כשיקויימו הדברים ויגיע קץ האמת ויבא משיחנו, אזי ידעו למפרע איך שמרומז בדבריו זמן הקץ, וכן מצינו בכמה נביאים.

ר' נחמן מברסלב, ליקוטי מוהר"ן קמא, סימן קפו.

ב) בת קול

1

תנו רבנן, משמתו נביאים האחרונים, חגי, זכריה ומלאכי, נסתלקה רוח הקודש מישראל, ואף־על־פי כן היו משתמשין בבת קול.

סנהדרין יא,א.

2

אמר רבי שפטיה אמר רבי יוחנן, מנין שמשתמשין בבת קול, שנאמר (ישעיה ל,כא) ואזניך תשמענה דבר מאחריך לאמר.

מגילה לב,א.

3

אמר רבי אלעזר, הולכין אחר שמיעת בת קול. מה טעמא? ואזניך תשמענה דבר מאחריך לאמר זה הדרך לכו בה (ישעיה ל,כא). בר קפרא היה איעלל לחדא קרייא. מי עלל נכשל באצבעו. עאל ושמע קליה דטלייא קרי, אם בגפו יבא בגפו יצא (שמות

כא,ג). אמר, דומה שלא עלת בידי אלא הטחה זו בלבד. וכן הוות ליה. רבי יוחנן ורבי שמעון בן לקיש הוי מתחמדין מיחמי אפוייי דשמואל. אמרין, נלך אחר שמיעת בת קול. עברין קומי סידרא, שמעין קליה דטלייא, ושמואל מת (שמואל א כח,ג) ,וסיימון. וכן הוות ליה. רבי יונה ורבי יוסה סלקין מבקרה לרבי אחא דהוה תשיש. אמרין, נלך בתר שמיעת בת קול. שמעין קליה דאיתתא אמרה לחבירתה, איטפי בוצינה? אמרה לה, לא יתטפי ולא מיטפי בוציניהון דישראל.

ירושלמי שבת ו,ט.

הוה איעלל – היה נכנס לכפר אחד. מי עלל – כשנכנס נכשל באצבעו. עאל – נכנס ושמע קול התינוקות קורין אם בגפו וכו'. הטחה זו – רק מכה זו לבדה. הוי מתחמדין – חשקה נפשם לראות לשמואל בבבל לשאול ממנו ספיקות שהיו להם. וסיימון – נטלו הדבר ההוא לסימן ולא ירדו לבבל לשמואל. סלקין לבקרא – עלו לבקר את רבי אחא שהיה חולה. איטפי בוצינא – דרך שאלה אמרה לחברתה אם כבה נרה. לא יתטפי – דרך צחות אמרה לא נתכבה ולא יתכבה נרן של ישראל.

פני משה, שם.

4

ועיין בזוהר, שלח קסט,א בסוד קלא דהדרא (=קול חוזר) . . . כי הנה ענין קלא דהדרא הוא הנקרא בת קול בלשון רז"ל, שאמרו במדרש (שמו"ר סו"פ כט) אדם יש לקולו בת קול, ועיין בתוספות פרק קמא דסנהדרין (יא,א) גבי משמתו נביאים אחרונים נסתלקה נבואה ועדיין משתמשים בבת קול. פירשו התוספות דבת קול היינו קלא דהדרא מקול השם יתברך, עיין שם. ובפרק קמא דבבא בתרא (יב,א) איתא ניטלה נבואה מן הנביאים וניתנה לחכמים ושם אחר-כך דניתנה לשוטים ולתינוקות. והאמת הכל אחד ורבותינו ז"ל בירושלמי, פרק במה אשה, גלו לנו בספורים שספרו שם עם הבת-קול שהיא שמיעת קול בני-אדם ממש

המדברים לעניניהם והם אין מתכוונים כלל לזה רק הוא השומע
יודע מזה למה שהוא צריך. וזה שלמדוהו שם מקרא דואזניך
תשמענה דבר מאחריך, וכן למדו בבבלי שילהי מגילה . . . פירוש
בסוד אחוריים דאין הזיווג והשפעות השם יתברך אלינו פנים
בפנים שנכיר ונדע איך השם יתברך הנותן ואנו מקבלים מיד ליד.
שזהו הנבואה במאמר כה אמר ד' שהיה מכיר בפירוש שהשם
יתברך מדבר עמו. אבל משחרב בית־המקדש נסתלקה ההכרה
דפנים־בפנים הזו לשמוע הדבור מלפניו רק מאחריו שהוא כטעם
כלאחר ידו. וכמו שכתבנו לעיל דאחוריים רוצה לומר מעללים
שאין האדם מתכוין להם והיינו כי השם יתברך משמיע אליו קולו
מרצונו דרך בני־אדם אלו שהם מתכוונים מעצמם ומכוונתם
לדבר זה לענין אחר. ואינו נמשך מכוונת השם יתברך בפירוש
ובהיכר ברור לכל רק כטעם מאחריו ובו היו משתמשים אז.
פירוש שעל כל כל דבר היו רואים או שומעים קול או פעולת אדם
אחד שלא נתכוון להם כלל וממנו היו יודעים לעניינם ולצרכם.
וכך היה השם יתברך מזמין להם על כל דבר שהיו צריכים וזהו
ההשתמשות בבת־קול כמו הנביאים על כל דבר שהיו צריכים היו
שומעים הקול ממש שהשם יתברך מדבר עמם לנוכח כך וכך פנים
בפנים, ומשמתו נביאים היה מדבר עמהם מאחריו והיינו קלא
דהדרא. כידוע בחכמת הטבע שבמקום אשר יפסוק הקול ויפגוש
באיזה דבר קשה, הקול מכה בו וחוזר ומשמיע קול הברה כאותו
קול. וחכמי הטבע בנו מגדלים שיהיו מחזירים הקולות זה לזה
כמה פעמים שהקול החוזר יחזור ויעשה קול החוזר ככתוב
בספריהם כי קול החוזר נשמע כאלו הוא קול בפני עצמו שמשמיע
אותו דבר ובאמת אינו אלא האחוריים דקול הראשון אך אינו
ניכר אלא לקול בפני עצמו.

וידוע, כל פעולות וכל דבורי בני־אדם הכל הוא מעצמות
השם יתברך, שהשם יתברך פועל ומדבר באותו רגע ענין זה. רק
שהוא כטעם ד' יתן אומר המבשרות צבא רב (תהלים סח,יב)
שבהתפשטות הוא מתפשט לכמה אנפין בכל נברא כפי מה שהוא
כלי קיבול להשמיע הקלא הדהדרא. [כידוע דקול החוזר הוא כפי
השתנות המשמיע אותו קול־החוזר בקשיותיו ועניינו כנודע
בחכמת הטבע]. שכל פעולות בני־אדם ודבורם הוא רק קלא
דהדרא מפעולות השם יתברך. דרך משל, כשהשם יתברך דבר
טוב, אז כל הברואים חפצים בטוב ומדברים מזה, רק כל אחד מה
שהוא אצלו טוב. אצל בני־ישראל מה שהוא אצלם טוב, ואצל

העכו"ם כל אומה ואומה לפי אופיה שלה, לזו עשירות ולזו ניאוף ולזו רציחה ולזו ממשלה וכיוצא, וכן אצל הבעלי־חיים לפי ענייניהם, וזה בכלל, וכן אצל כל פרט ופרט, והנה לכן אי־אפשר כלל לעמוד על אמיתות קולו של השם יתברך ורצונו מאחר שניתן עליו גם־כן דעת בני־אדם ומשתנה אצל כל אחד ואחד רק למשתמשים בבת־קול והוא קול גברא במתא כנזכר לעיל [קול גברא במתא הוא קול שאינו שכיח ודבר שאין שכיח ודאי הוא הזדמנות השם יתברך לאיזה דבר — ב.נ.]. כטעם מאי דקמן שמכיר היטב שזהו קלא דהדרא מקול השם יתברך אליו. או שוטים ותינוקות שאין להם דעת עצמם עדיין וקולם הוא אחוריים דקול השם יתברך שהוא הקלא דהדרא. [ואין קושיה מעתה איך סלקא דעתך שתהיה הנבואה רק לאלו החסרי דעת, שוטים ותינוקות. רק כי באמת הקלא דהדרא הוא אצל כל כל אדם, רק שכל אחד שיש בו דעת, הקול משתנה כפי דעתו כנזכר לעיל, עד שאין ניכר אמיתותו. מה שאין כן בשוטה ותינוקת הם כלים פשוטים שהקלא דהדרא שלהם הוא בלי כוונת מכוונת כלל ולכן הוא קלא דהדרא ברור].

וגם־כן לחכמים, פירוש חכמי ישראל האמיתים היודעים ומכירים שכל חכמתם מהשם יתברך. ומכל מקום, אינו פנים בפנים ממש כמו הנביאים שהיו יודעים בבירור גמור עד שיוכלו לומר כה אמר ד' על נביעות חכמתם כי לא היה נובע כלל מפי עצמם רק שומעים קול ד'. אבל חכמי ישראל, החכמה נובעת מלב עצמם, רק שהוא קלא דהדרא מקול השם יתברך, דעל־ידי קול השם יתברך נולד בהם אותו קול דדברי חכמה. והוא נדמה כאלו קול עצמם הוא ובאמת אינו אלא קול השם יתברך, רק שהוא אינו משיג הפנים דקול אלא האחוריים כשחוזר מתוך לב הבן־אדם ושנראה כאלו קול זה מתחדש ממנו. [ובכלל התורה־שבכתב הוא קול השם יתברך כמפורש בכתוב קולות. והתורה שבעל־פה הוא הקלא דהדרא מקול דתורה־שבכתב. וקלא דהדרא של חכמי המשנה חזר והוליד קול החוזר של בעלי התלמוד. וקולם חזר והוליד קלא דהדרא של חכמי ישראל שאחריהם, והכל הוא רק נמשך מראשית הקול של השם יתברך בתורה־שבכתב, רק שהקלא דהדרא מתגלגל וחוזר כמה פעמים, כמו שכתבנו לעיל מחכמת הטבע גם־כן].

ר' צדוק הכהן מלובלין, דובר צדק, עא, ד־עב, ג.

5

כי כל העולם הזה, הוא התלבשות מדריגות התחתונות של הקדושה, היינו בחינת רגלין של הקדושה, בבחינת (ישעיה סו, א) והארץ הדום רגלי. [אף שגם מדריגות העליונות של הקדושה, יש מהם גם־כן התגלות בעולם הזה. אך שאין ההתגלות מתלבש בעצם בזה העולם, כי־אם הארה שמאיר בבחינת רגלין. אבל בחינת רגלין, מתגלין בעצם בזה העולם.] וכל יום יש בו מחשבה דיבור ומעשה, והקדוש ברוך הוא מצמצם אלוקותו מאין סוף עד אין תכלית. עד נקודת המרכז של עולם הגשמי שעומד עליו, ומזמין לו לכל אדם מחשבה דיבור ומעשה, לפי היום ולפי האדם ולפי המקום. ומלביש לו בזאת המחשבה דיבור ומעשה שמזמין לו, רמזים כדי לקרבו לעבודתו. בכן צריך להעמיק מחשבתו בזה, ולהגדיל בינתו, ולהבין מהי הרמיזות בפרטיות, שמלובשת בזאת המחשבה דיבור ומעשה של זה היום, שהזמין לו השם יתברך. הן מלאכה או משא־ומתן, וכל מה שמזמין לו השם יתברך בכל יום, צריך להעמיק ולהגדיל מחשבתו בזה, כדי להבין רמיזותיו של השם יתברך.

ר׳ נחמן מברסלב, ליקוטי מוהר״ן קמא, נד, ב.

ג

הנבואה / עתיד

"האדם חפשי בדמיונו, ואסור במושכלו"
— ר' ישראל מסאלאנט, אגרת המוסר

1

דע כי אמתת הנבואה ומהותה הוא שפע שופע מאת השם
יתברך . . . על הכח הדברי (=השכל) בתחלה, ואחר כך ישפע על כח
המדמה (=הדמיון), וזאת היא היותר עליונה שבמדרגות האדם
ותכלית השלימות אשר אפשר שימצא למינו, והענין ההוא הוא
תכלית שלימות הכח המדמה, וזה ענין אי אפשר בכל איש בשום
פנים ואינו ענין יגיעו אליו בשלימות בחכמות העיוניות והטבת
המדות, ואפילו יהיו כלם בתכלית מה שיוכלו להיות מן הטוב
והנאה שבהם, עד שיחובר אליו שלימות הכח המדמה בעקר
היצירה בתכלית מה שאפשר.

רבי משה בר מיימון, מורה הנבוכים, ב, לו.

17

2

תדע שזה השפע השכלי כשיהיה שופע על הכוח הדברי לבד, ולא ישפע דבר ממנו על הכח המדמה, אם למעוט הדבר השופע או לחסרון היה במדמה בעקר הבריאה ולא יוכל לקבל שפע השכל, שזה הוא כת החכמים בעלי העיון, וכשיהיה השפע ההוא על שני הכחות יחד, רוצה לומר, הדברי והמדמה על תכלית שלימותם ביצירה, זהו כת הנביאים, ואם יהיה השפע על המדמה לבד ויהיה קצר הדברי, אם מעקר היצירה או למעוט התלמדות, זאת הכת הם מנהיגי המדינות, מניחי הנימוסים, והקוסמים, והמנחשים, ובעלי החלומות הצודקים, וכן העושים הפליאות בתחבולות הזרות והמלאכות הנעלמות, עם היותם בלתי חכמים הם כלם מזאת הכת השלישית. [הדגשה שלי—ב.נ.]

רבי משה בר מיימון, מורה הנבוכים, ב, לז.

3

וכבר ידעת כי כל כח גופני יחלש וילאה ויפסד עת, ויבריא עת אחרת, וזה הכח המדמה כח גופני בלא ספק, ולזה תמצא הנביאים תתבטל נבואתם בעת האבל או בעת הכעס וכיוצא בהם, כבר ידעת אמרתם אין הנבואה שורה לא מתוך עצבות ולא מתוך עצלות, ושיעקב אבינו לא באתהו נבואה כל ימי אבלו, להתעסק כחו המדמה בהפקד יוסף, ושמשה רבינו, עליו השלום, לא באתהו הנבואה כבואה מקדם מאחר תלונת המרגלים עד שמתו כל דור המדבר אנשי המלחמה, בעבור שנלאה לסבלם לרוב תלונותיהם . . . וכן עוד תמצא קצת הנביאים נבאו מדת זמן אחת ואחר כן נפסקה הנבואה מהם ולא התמידה להם בעבור מקרה שנתחדש, וזאת היא הסבה העצמית הקרובה בהפסק הנבואה בזמן הגלות בלא ספק, כלומר עצלות או עצבות שיהיה לאדם בענין מן הענינים, ויותר רע מזה היותו עבד נקנה נעבד לסכלים הזונים, אשר קבצו העדר הדבר האמתי ותגבורת כל התאוות הבהמיות ואין לאל ידו, ובזה יעדנו רע והוא אשר רצה באמרו,

ישוטטו לבקש את דבר ה' ולא ימצאו (עמוס ח,יב), ואמר מלכה
ושריה בגוים אין תורה גם נביאיה לא מצאו חזון מה' (איכה ב,ט),
וזה אמת מבואר העלה כי הכלי כבר נתבטל, והוא הסבה גם כן
בשוב הנבואה לנו על מנהגה לימות המשיח, מהרה יגלה כמו
שיעד.

רבי משה בר מיימון, מורה הנבוכים, ב, לו.

4

דע שיש אור, שהוא למעלה מנפשין ורוחין ונשמתין, והוא
אור אין סוף. ואף על־פי שאין השכל משיג אותו, אף על־פי כן
רדיפה דמחשבה למירדף אבתריה (=לרדוף אחריו). ועל־ידי
הרדיפה, אז השכל משיג אותו בבחינת מטי־ולא־מטי (=מגיע ולא
מגיע). כי באמת אי אפשר להשיג אותו, כי הוא למעלה מנר"ן
(=נפש, רוח, נשמה). . . .

וכשעושה ומתקן את המיישב והמסדר שהוא הכתר כראוי,
והמוחין רודפין להשיג האור אין סוף. והכתר מעכב את השכל,
כדי ליישב את השכל. ועל־ידי הרדיפה והמעכב, אזי מכה המוחין
במיישב והמסדר, ונעשין היכלין לאור אין סוף. . . .

[הכתר הוא המיישב והמסדר את המוחין, דהיינו הכח שיש
בשכל של אדם ליישב ולסדר את המוח והדעת לבל יהרוס לצאת
חוץ מן הגבול, זה הכח הוא בחינת כתר כנזכר לעיל. וזה הכח הוא
כמו מחיצה המפסקת בין המוחין ובין האור אין סוף, כי זה הכח
שהוא המיישב והמסדר, הוא מעכב את המוחין בעת מרוצתם
ורדיפתם לבל יהרסו לעלות אל ה' למעלה ממחיצתם, כי המוחין
רודפין להשיג האור אין סוף. וזה הכח הנזכר לעיל של השכל
שהוא המיישב והמסדר, שהוא בחינת כתר, הוא עומד בפניהם
כמו מחיצה, ומעכב אותם מרדיפתם כנ"ל. ועל־ידי הרדיפה
והמעכב, היינו על־ידי הרדיפה שהמוחין רודפין להשיג אור האין
סוף, ועל־ידי הכח המעכב, שהוא כח המיישב והמסדר, בחינת
כתר כנ"ל, על־ידי שתי בחינות אלו, על־ידי זה מבטשין ומכין
המוחין בבחינת המחיצה הנ"ל שהוא המיישב והמסדר, ועל־ידי
זה נעשין היכלין לאור אין סוף. דהיינו שנעשין בחינת כלים
והיכלות ברוחניות עליון, להשיג על ידם בבחינת מטי־ולא־מטי

אור האין סוף, ברוך הוא. כי אם לא היה המעכב הנ"ל כלל, ולא היה מי שיעכב את המוחין מרדיפתם ומרוצתם, היו מתבטלין המוחין לגמרי. כי היה האדם מתבטל במציאות, כי אור האין סוף אי־אפשר להשיג. אך על־ידי שתי הבחינות, שהן הרדיפה והמעכב, על־ידי זה נעשין בחינת מחיצות והיכלין הנ"ל שעל ידם משיגין אור האין סוף רק בבחינת מטי־ולא־מטי. ופירוש מטי־ולא־מטי, ידוע למבינים, דהיינו שמגיע ואינו מגיע, שרודף ומגיע להשיג ואף על־פי כן אינו מגיע ומשיג].

ר' נחמן מברסלב, ליקוטי מוהר"ן קמא, כד.

5

באמת ישראל רחוקים לגמרי מעבודה זרה כי ישראל בכלל הם בבחינת הארת הגוונין בבחינת אור השכל האמת דקדושה והעכו"ם הם בבחינת כח המדמה כי יש באדם כח השכל וכח המדמה. וזה הכח המדמה הוא גם־כן כח מהשכל דהיינו כח התחתון של השכל שהוא הכח המדמה והמצייר בדעתו כל הדברים הגשמיים וכל המלאכות והוא מביא כולם לתוך המוח והשכל. ומי שיש לו כח השכל האמתי הוא צריך להגביר השכל על המדמה דהיינו שיפשיט כל דבר מגשמיותו ויבין מתוכו גדולת הבורא יתברך עד שיפשיט דעתו מגשמיות הדבר שנצטייר בדעתו שהוא בחינת המדמה וישוב לכח השכל האמת לכלול באין סוף שהוא הבורא יתברך. כי זה עיקר השכל האמת לדעת ולהכיר אותו יתברך לבטל כח המדמה המלובש בגשמיות העשיה ולעלות אל השגת השכל האמתי להכיר את הבורא יתברך שהוא למעלה מכל התמונות והדמיונות שבכח המדמה שממנו נמשכין כולם כי כל התמונות והדמיונות נמשכין מהאין סוף שאין בו תמונה.

ר' נתן מנמירוב, ליקוטי הלכות, הלכות עבודת אלילים, ג, ב.

6

יהיה שפיכת הרוח לכל בשר בהשפעת הנבואה וחזיונות לכנסת ישראל שהוא על־ידי קדושת הירכין דנצח והוד דמשם יניקת הנביאים . . . ודבר זה רק על־ידי שלימות קדושת הברית שהוא קדושת הירכין.

ר' צדוק הכהן מלובלין, פוקד עקרים, יד, ד.

7

החסידות האחרונה פנתה אל הרגש והדמיון יותר מאל השכל והמעשה, ובשביל כך העירה הרבה את תביעת הטהרה הבשרית.

ראי"ה קוק, אורות, עמ' פא.

8

אם יתפאר המדע החדש שהשתחרר מהתיאולוגיה, צריך הוא לדעת, שלעומת זה נשתחררה התיאולוגיה מהמדע, שאסרה בכבלים אנושיים. אמנם ודאי שם חדש ייקרא להענין העליון, לא שם אשר אנשים יצרוהו, כי־אם שם חדש אשר פי ד' יקבנו. התיאולוגיה המשוחררת מכבלי המדע היא הנבואה, סגולתן של ישראל, שתיגלה עלינו במהרה.

ראי"ה קוק, ערפלי טוהר (ירוש' ה'תשמ"ג) עמ' מ.

9

כל התרבות הזמנית בנויה היא על יסוד כח המדמה. זוהי מורשת גורלם האלילי של עמי התרבות האחוזים בכח המדמה, שממנו באה התפתחות היופי הגופני בפועל ובציור מעשי. הולך ומשתכלל כח המדמה, ועמו משתכללים המדעים המעשיים והנסיוניים, ועל-פי עליתו של כח המדמה ותפיסתו את החיים מסתלק האור השכלי, מפני שחושב העולם כולו שכל האושר תלוי בפתוחו של כח המדמה. וכה הולכים העניינים בהדרגה, עד ששרידי השכל שברוח החכמה החולונית גם הם הולכים ונעתקים אל כח המדמה. המליצים והמספרים, הדרמתוריים וכל העוסקים באמנויות היפות נוטלים מקום בראש התרבות, והפילוסופיה פוסחת וצולעת ואין לה מעמד מפני שהשכל הנקי הולך ומסתלק. כפי סלוקו של השכל ורוח החכמה, כן חוצפא יסגי וחכמת סופרים תסרח, יראי חטא ימאסו והאמת היא נעדרת ופני הדור כפני כלב . . . אמנם כל-זה הוא יסוד עצה מרחוק, עצת ד' היא להשלים את כח המדמה, מפני שהוא בסיס בריא לרוח העליון שיופיע עליו, ומתוך העליונות של התפיסה הרוחנית שקדמה בישראל הוכרח כח המדמה להתמוגג, מה שגרם חלישות לאחיזת רוח-הקדש העליון, שעתיד לבא על-ידי מלכא משיחא. על-כן מתבסס כעת רוח המדמה עד שיגמר בכל תיאורו, ואז יהיה כסא נכון ושלם לרוח ד' העליון ויוכשר לקבל אור רוח הקודש עליו, שהוא רוח ד' "רוח חכמה ובינה, רוח עצה וגבורה רוח דעת ויראת ד'" (ישעיה יא,ב).

ראי"ה קוק, אורות, עמ' לד-לה.

10

איך אפשר להתרפא מאותם הדמיונות המתעים? גם על השאלה הזו נותנת החסידות תשובה פשוטה מאד, ואומרת: על-ידי דמיונות אחרים אמתיים. ראוי לנו להתרגל מיד בימי נעורינו לעבוד בכח-הדמיון שבנו, לפתחו ולהשלימו, כדי שיהיה אפשר לנו לצייר בשכלנו דמיונות אחרים אמתיים ולהחליש בקרבנו באופן זה מעט-מעט את דמיונות השוא המטעים ולהתרפא מהם . . .

מתחלה נבאר את הדמיון המאיר לנו ופותח את עינינו,
לראות את מצבנו וערכנו האמתי בעולם ושפלותנו הנוראה. כדי
להגיע לזה ראוי להתחיל באופן זה: ראשית כל נשתדל לצייר לנו
בשכלנו ובכח-הדמיון שבנו את כדור-הארץ, ונדמה לנו כאלו
רואים אנחנו מרחוק את כדור-הארץ כולו עם כל חמשת חלקי
התבל אשר עליו ואת כל הימים המקיפים אותם. נצייר לנו גם את
כל העמים הדרים בכל חלקי התבל לשלונותיהם ולגבולותיהם,
ואת מספר האנשים של כל אומה ולשון. את כל זה נצייר לנו
היטב, כאלו אנו רואים את המחזה הזה לפנינו ממש, בחוש-
הראיה הגשמי שלנו. בתחלה לא יפעול עלינו הדמיון הזה הרבה כי
הלא חדש הוא עודנו אצלינו. כח דמיוננו עדיין חלש הוא, כי עוד
לא השתמשנו בו עד עכשיו כל צרכו, אולם במשך הזמן, אם נשקוד
על הדבר בהתמדה ונתרגל לעבודה זו יום-יום בלי הפסק,
ולפעמים אם יהיה אפשר לנו, גם פעמים ביום, אזי נראה זאת,
בעינינו הרוחניות ועיני שכלנו, תמיד ביתר ברירות וביתר
בהירות, כאלו אפשר היה למשמש במראה זו בידים.
לא רק את האנשים נצייר לנו, כי אם גם את שאר הנבראים
הנמצאים בעולם, היינו את כל הבהמות והחיות שנדע אותן, היכן
הן נמצאות ומה מראיהן וטבען, את המון החיות הטורפות
שבמדבריות ויערות, האיך הן טורפות ואוכלות, את המון
הבהמות הביתיות שבין בני-אדם, האיך הם משתמשים בהן
ונהנים מהן, את המון שאר מיני הנבראים היותר קטנים כמו
היתושים, והיותר גדולים כמו הפילים, את הנחשים ושאר מיני
שקצים ורמשים, איך הם רוחשים בארץ, הולכים, רצים, נחים,
אוכלים, נבראים ומתים. את כל מיני העופות הפורחים, את המון
מיני הצפצופים והנגינות, שהם מצפצפים ומנגנים באויר,
באילנות, בשדות ובכרמים, את המון מיני הדגים שבימים ונהרות,
האיך הם שטים, נבלעים, נולדים, נצודים ומתים. את כל מיני
הצמחים, התבואות, הירקות, העשבים, החוחים והפרחים רבי-
הגונים, הגנות, הפרדסים, השדות הכרמים והיערות. את כל אותם
הדברים כפי מה שאנו יודעים אותם מה מראיתם, איך הם
פורחים, נפתחים, גדלים, מתיבשים, נכמשים, נופלים ונחלפים.
את כל זאת נצייר לנו באר היטב, כל דבר בפרט על מקומו, ובדרך
כלל הכל ביחד, כפי מה שראינו אותם, או קראנו ולמדנו אודותם.
אחרי זמן ידוע, כאשר — לפי טבע האדם ולפי השקידה —
כבר יבורר לנו הדבר הזה היטב, אחרי אשר נראה את הציורים

האלה בבהירות כה זכה, עד שנתפעל מהם בנפשנו ונרגיש בחוש איך המחזה היפה הזה פועל עלינו ומקסים אותנו, כמו האדם המתפעל מהדר הטבע אשר רואה בעיניו הגשמיות, אזי נלך הלאה וננסה לצייר לנו את המקום אשר אנחנו עומדים עליו עכשיו, ונשתדל להציג את עצמנו בין המון כל אותם בני־האדם והמון כל אותם הברואים. מתחלה יקשה לנו הדבר מאד לצייר לנו ציור כזה כי כל ישותנו וכל חשיבותנו הדמיונית שנטבעה בנפשנו תתקומם נגדנו ולא תתן לנו בשום אופן להאבד ולהבטל בין המון כל אותן הבריות, לא תתן לנו בשום אופן לותר על גאותנו המדומה, ולראות את האמת האי־נעימה כל־כך, שהיא שפלותנו וקטנותנו הנוראה. אולם ההרגל יעשה את שלו, ובמשך הזמן יעלה בידינו להתגבר על כל המניעות, ויקל לנו תמיד יותר לצייר לנו בכח דמיוננו את הציור הנפלא הזה.

ר' מנחם עקשטיין, תנאי הנפש להשגת החסידות (וינה, תרפ"א) עמ' ב־ד.

ד

קוסמולוגיות חזיוניות

א) מעשה מרכבה

וארא והנה רוח סערה באה מן הצפון ענן גדול ואש
מתלקחת ונגה לו סביב ומתוכה כעין החשמל מתוך האש. ומתוכה
דמות ארבע חיות וזה מראיהן דמות אדם להנה. וארבעה פנים
לאחת וארבע כנפים לאחת להם.

יחזקאל א, ד-ו.

וארבעה אפין לחדא, וארבע אפין לכל חד וחד, שתת־עסר
אפין לבריתא חדא, מנין אפיא דארבע ברין שתין־וארבעא אפין,
וארבעה גפין לחדא וארבעה גפין לכל חד וחד, שתת־עסר גפין
לכל אפא ואפא, שתין־וארבעא גפין לבריתא חדא, והוו מנין
גפיא דארבע ברין מאתן־וחמשין־ושתא גפין.

תרגום שם, פסוק ו.

וארבעה פנים לאחת — לאחת זו לפרצוף האדם לבדה היו
ארבעה פנים וכן לאריה ולנשר ולשור הרי שש־עשרה לחיה, וכן

25

לכל חיה וחיה, וארבעה כנפים לכל אחד מן הפנים, הרי ששים־
וארבע כנפים לחיה.

רש"י שם.

דעת לנבון נקל כי במעשה מרכבה של יחזקאל הנביא
מדובר בפרוגרסיה גיאומטרית (הנדסית): ארבע כפול ארבע
כפול ארבע כפול ארבע. האם יש כאן מעין ביטוי מתמטי לטעם
אין־סוף?

ב) מקור משלי האר"י ז"ל ותורותיו במה שנקראת "חויה אכסטטית"

ולרמח"ל, ענין זה במראה נראה הצמצום, כמו שיש בצפית
המרכבה מראה ופתרון, דהיינו ראיה והבנה.

ר' דוד כהן, קול הנבואה, עמ' ריג, על־פי קל"ח פתחי חכמה לרמח"ל, פתח כד
בעניין הצמצום, פירוש.

כל זה כעניין מראות ישעיה ויחזקאל, והיינו צפיית המרכבה,
שרואים אותה בסדריה ומבינים בה גדולת הנהגת יתברך שמו.

ר' משה חיים לוצאטו, ביאורים לספר אוצרות חיים, אות א (ועיי"ש אות יח),
נדפס בגנזי רמח"ל (בני ברק, תש"מ), עמ' רצז.

ולא זו הדרך שהשיג האריז"ל אותם הדברים, שהדבר ידוע
שהוא לא המציא לו משלים להלביש דבריו דאם־כן למה בחר לו
במשליו האלה, גם ודאי צריך בילוי זמן עצום לזה לחקור איך
להלביש דברים במשל שיהיה מכוון לנמשל, אבל כל השגותיו היו

דרך צפייה בנסתרות והוא ראה כל המראה הזה כדרך שראה
יחזקאל המרכבה.

ר' צדוק הכהן, ספר הזכרונות (נספח ל-דברי סופרים) לא,ב.

(ג) הורת תורותיו המתמטיות של ר' שם-טוב גפן בחזון

הופיע פתאום כמו אור גדול לנגד עיני הכואבות וממדים
לאין-ספור התייצבו לנגד עיני רוחי, כשעיני בשר שלי היו סגורות,
והיה נדמה לי כמו שחשתי את הממדים הרבים בחושי ממש, פעם
ולא יסף, והתהלכתי בתוכם.

ר' שם-טוב גפן, הממדים-הנבואה-האדמתנות (ירוש' תשל"ד) עמ' כז-כח,
"מזיכרונותיי".